Using Declarative Mapping Sentences in Psychological Research

Using facet theory and Hackett's pioneering development of the declarative mapping sentence (DMS) as a qualitative methodology, this volume explains the process of formulating and applying the DMS to critically assess female representation in science fiction.

Using a comparative approach to the development of female roles in Western science fiction films and television, the authors illustrate how the DMS is formulated and used to analyse the psychological and behavioural profiles of female characters. By maintaining the common structure of the DMS across films while adapting its content for each female role, the text demonstrates the flexibility of the DMS in providing a structure for varied research domains, enabling results to be uniformly compared, contrasted and classified.

This insightful and thought-provoking volume will appeal to researchers, academics and educators interested in psychological methods and statistics, qualitative research in gender identity, and research methods more generally. Those especially interested in behavioural psychology, gender and cinema, and science fiction will also benefit from this volume.

Paul M. W. Hackett is Professor of Ethnography and Research Methods at Emerson College, USA, Visiting Professor in the Department of Philosophy, Nnamdi Azikiwe University, Awka, Nigeria, Visiting Professor of Health Research Methods at University of Suffolk, UK, and Visiting Scholar at Royal Anthropological Institute, UK. He is the author of *Facet Theory and the Mapping Sentence*, second edition (2021), and *Declarative Mapping Sentence in Qualitative Research* (2021), and a co-author of *An Introduction to Using Mapping Sentences* (2021).

Chenwei Li completed her master's degree in Strategic Communication for Marketing in the School of Communication, Emerson College, USA, and her bachelor's degree in Film and Media Studies in the School of Humanity, University of California Irvine, USA.

Routledge Research in Psychology

This series offers an international forum for original and innovative research being conducted across the field of psychology. Titles in the series are empirically or theoretically informed and explore a range of dynamic and timely issues and emerging topics. The series is aimed at upper-level and post-graduate students, researchers, and research students, as well as academics and scholars.

Recent titles in the series include:

The Psychological Basis of Moral Judgments
Philosophical and Empirical Approaches to Moral Relativism
John J. Park

Developing a Model of Islamic Psychology and Psychotherapy
Islamic Theology and Contemporary Understandings of Psychology
Abdallah Rothman

Human Interaction with the Divine, the Sacred, and the Deceased
Psychological, Scientific, and Theological Perspectives
Edited by Thomas G. Plante and Gary E. Schwartz

Developing a Foundation for Learning with Internationally Adopted Children
Family-Based Activities for Remedial Learning and Attachment
Boris Gindis and Carol S. Lidz

Using Declarative Mapping Sentences in Psychological Research
Applying Facet Theory in Multi-Componential Critical Analyses of Female Representation in Science Fiction Film and TV
Paul M. W. Hackett and Chenwei Li

For a complete list of titles in this series, please visit: www.routledge.com/ Routledge-Research-in-Psychology/book-series/RRIP

Using Declarative Mapping Sentences in Psychological Research

Applying Facet Theory in Multi-Componential Critical Analyses of Female Representation in Science Fiction Film and TV

Paul M. W. Hackett and Chenwei Li

Routledge
Taylor & Francis Group

NEW YORK AND LONDON

First published 2022
by Routledge
605 Third Avenue, New York, NY 10158

and by Routledge
4 Park Square, Milton Park, Abingdon, Oxon, OX14 4RN

Routledge is an imprint of the Taylor & Francis Group, an informa business

© 2022 Paul M. W. Hackett and Chenwei Li

The right of Paul M. W. Hackett and Chenwei Li to be identified as authors of this work has been asserted in accordance with sections 77 and 78 of the Copyright, Designs and Patents Act 1988.

Library of Congress Cataloging-in-Publication Data
Names: Hackett, Paul, 1960- author. | Li, Chenwei, author.
Title: Using declarative mapping sentences in psychological research : applying facet theory in multi-componential critical analyses of female representation in science fiction film and television / Paul M. W. Hackett and Chenwei Li.
Description: 1 Edition. | New York, NY : Routledge, 2022. | Series: Routledge research in psychology | Includes bibliographical references and index.
Identifiers: LCCN 2021057816 | ISBN 9780367686499 (hardback) | ISBN 9780367686512 (paperback) | ISBN 9781003138419 (ebook)
Subjects: LCSH: Gender identity—Research. | Women—Psychology. | Science fiction—Psychological aspects. | Social psychology. | Qualitative research.
Classification: LCC HQ18.55 .H34 2022 | DDC 305.3—dc23/eng/ 20220217 LC record available at https://lccn.loc.gov/2021057816

ISBN: 978-0-367-68649-9 (hbk)
ISBN: 978-0-367-68651-2 (pbk)
ISBN: 978-1-003-13841-9 (ebk)

DOI: 10.4324/9781003138419

Typeset in Times New Roman
by Apex CoVantage, LLC

Paul's dedication: Paul would like to thank Chenwei for the hard work and inspiration she has put into this research and writing. Paul would like to dedicate this book to Jessica and to all of those people who were at the front of the line to receive Covid-19 inoculations. These people did not "wait to see" what would happen after the injections were given. They did not let others take the risk for them. They did not deny the science. They were courageous and possessed basic decency and a community spirit. If we overcome Covid-19 we must thank these people along with all the scientists and many other professionals.

Chenwei's dedication: To Paul, for being the most selfless professor and a genuine friend of mine. It has been a fantastic experience working with you.

To my parents, for always being there for me.

To people, who are looking forward to defeat Covid-19. Do have hope. We will get through this together.

Contents

Tables

Figures

Preface

Last year, 2020, will be remembered for many things, including: the UK general election at the end of 2019 that ratified the Brexit vote in the UK, the Covid-19 pandemic and the Black Lives Matter movement. The latter two of these will now be briefly reflected upon, as they relate to the contents of this book.

Black Lives Matter

The focus of our writing is upon gender in science fiction, although we must comment upon the Black Lives Matter movement and the racist events of 2020. During that year, there were many racist events that made a significant impact around the world. Among these, two stood out: the killing of George Floyd and the unfounded and racist accusation of an attack made against bird watcher and a person of colour, Christian Cooper, by a white woman in Central Park, New York City. The Black Lives Matter movement had arisen before these atrocities, but it was given added impetus by them. However, it is a year since these incidents, and in this time, black people have continued to be killed and injured by white police officers and other white people.

This book is about the analysis of characters in science fiction movie media. Science fiction is notorious for its eclectic use of mind-bending special effects and the inclusion of creatures from alien worlds: the films and programmes we have selected exemplify such features. Our research has a bias towards Western forms of science fiction and movies and television from this region which has, in the twentieth century, been typified by its use of human characters who are predominantly white. The character of Lieutenant Uhura in Star Trek is a very early example of a person of colour within a science fiction television programme. It should be noted though that while the casting of a black woman in a mainstream US television programme was somewhat ground breaking, the role was still one that assisted white men. We discuss this role at much greater length in the book. We also consider the positioning of people of colour in the final piece we evaluate which is a much more contemporary Star Trek episode.

However, neither of us (the authors of this book) is black, and as is typical of so much literature about racial representation, we write from a non-black perspective.

It is also of extreme importance that, as researchers, we attempt to acknowledge and declare our biases and prejudices and that none of us remain silent to individual and institutional acts of racism. As researchers, we may be placed in a situation where we are attempting to be neutral and to not make an impact upon the people or the subject matter we are investigating. This raises questions that we all have to answer regarding the extent to which being a researcher absolves us from attempting to right that which is wrong. Fortunately, neither of us encountered overtly racist depictions during the current research, but we may now have been sensitive to some possible forms of discrimination that were present in the movies and television programmes we watched. We would welcome feedback from readers if they feel that this is the case.

Covid-19

The impacts upon conducting research in the social sciences and humanities due to the Covid-19 pandemic have been commented upon by many including the first author (Hackett and Schwarzenbach, 2020). However, the virus has had a specific effect upon the research and writing of this book. We started both the research and our authorship of the book when we were living in the United States. Three months after the pandemic broke out, Chenwei returned to her home in Beijing, China. The planning of the research using a declarative mapping sentence to guide our explorations had been completed in its initial form when Chenwei made this move. The final parts of the research and all of the writing have, however, been undertaken inter-continentally via emails and video-conferencing calls. The 12-hour difference in time between the two countries dictated the times at which we met. It was, however, a very interesting and informative learning experience that we plan to repeat in the future.

Positionality Statement

Our positionality statement is closely related to what we have written in the previous two sections. The two authors of this book also conducted the research that underpins it. We approach this research and writing from different academic disciplines, namely psychology, ethnography and fine art (PH) and film studies and marketing (CL). It is important to consider our joint positionality, as this relates to the contents of our research. It is of special importance that our main reason for conducting this research and writing this book was due to our belief in the utility of employing a critical multifaceted approach to the analysis of films and television programmes. The experience of the first author in the application of the facet theory approach within the analysis of qualitative information, and especially in the discipline of fine art, predisposed him to consider using such an approach with movie media, while the experiences of the second author within the academic discipline of film studies brought a different perspective to this endeavour.

It is also important to stress that we take a critical position in the sense that we adopt a critical lens through which we inspect data and interpret our finding. This positionality is inevitably influential in our research, as we will consider the role of social structure and systems of discrimination as being pertinent in understanding the role of women in science fiction films and television productions and we will assume such structures to possess valency in our arriving at our interpretivist results.

Perhaps of central importance in our joint work has been the belief that an interpretivist position can successfully be untied with a flexible positivist outlook to allow the discussion of the blending of these outlooks (Hayre et al., 2021). We also come from very different physical locations and have grown up and lived in extremely different cultures [UK and USA (PH); China and USA (CL)]. There is also a difference in our ages where one of us remembers the original Star Trek airing (PH) and the other does not (CL). Such differences open up a philosophical discourse into our ontological and epistemological viewpoints which, we believe, adds to the richness of our analyses. We consider that the use of the mapping sentence as a guide to our research and analyses has helped us to frame our different perspectives in a way that allows the unification of our two, very different, voices. This has resulted in the facet theory approach being positioned as a tool that has the potential to analyse, from within an interpretivist perspective, qualitative information that arises from watching films and television using a more positivist framework that allows for a comparison between the different media analysed (Hayre et al., 2021).

Having considered some of the background features that underlie our writing and research, we now present a brief synopsis of the content of the book.

Chapter Synopsis

In the first chapter, we commence by considering the substantive area of research that we will be reporting upon, that of the genre of science fiction, as it has been portrayed both in films and in television. We also introduce the reader to the methodology we use in this research, that of facet theory (Canter, 1985; Hackett, 2021a) and the critical use of the declarative mapping sentence (Hackett, 2020; Hackett and Schwarzenbach, 2020). This approach will be employed in its qualitative form (Cowle and Hackett, 2021; Hackett, 2021b) and we take some time to present a background to this approach with the examples of its use. We will also set out what we mean by a critical approach, what it embodies in the critical paradigm and how this will in many ways determine our research and results.

The reviews and analyses of the four films we have chosen for this research are presented in Chapters 3–6. These chapters will address the following films and television programmes: Chapter 1 – Star Trek: The Original Series (episode 1: The Man Trap); Chapter 2 – Blade Runner; Chapter 3 –Ex Machina: Star Trek; Chapter 4 – Star Trek: Discovery (episode 1: The Vulcan Hello).

Having reviewed all the four films, in our final chapter, we contrast and compare the films and television programmes we have analysed. We use the initial declarative mapping sentence to guide our review. The critical use of the declarative mapping sentence also forms a conclusion that allows direct comparison between the four very different media offerings we considered. Finally, we consider the declarative mapping sentence in the development of a critical positioning and understanding of female character roles in science fiction films and television in terms of how this may be used to guide further research in this and other areas.

References

Canter, D. (ed.) (1985) *Facet Theory: Approaches to Social Research*, New York: Springer Verlag.

Cowle, K., and Hackett, P.M.W. (2021) Declarative Mapping Sentence Method for Investigating the Perception of Fine-Art Photographs for Individuals with Cerebral Visual Impairment, *Academia Letters*, Article 1173, https://doi.org/10.20935/AL1173

Hackett, P.M.W. (2014) *Facet Theory and the Mapping Sentence: Evolving Philosophy, Use and Applications*, Basingstoke: Palgrave McMillan Publishers.

Hackett, P.M.W. (2020) *Declarative Mapping Sentences in Qualitative Research: Theoretical, Linguistic, and Applied Usages*, London: Routledge.

Hackett, P.M.W. (2021) *Facet Theory and the Mapping Sentence: Evolving Philosophy, Use and Declarative Applications* (second, revised and enlarged edition), Basingstoke: Palgrave McMillan Publishers.

Hackett, P.M.W. (2021a) *Facet Theory and the Mapping Sentence: Evolving Philosophy, Use and Declarative Applications* (second, revised and enlarged edition), Basingstoke: Palgrave McMillan Publishers.

Hackett, P.M.W. (2021b) A Reflexive and Adaptable Framework for Ethnographic and Qualitative Research: the Declarative Mapping Sentences Approach, *Academia Letters*, https://doi.org/10.20935/AL999

Hackett, P.M.W., and Schwarzenbach, J.B. (2020) Black Lives Matter: Birdwatching in Central Park and the Murder of George Floyd, in Hackett, P.M.W., and Hayre, C. (eds.) *Handbook of Ethnography in Healthcare Research*, 15:1–7. doi: 10.1080/13648470.2021.1893657. Epub ahead of print. PMID: 34523375. London: Routledge.

Hayre, C.M., Muller, D., Sim, J., and Hackett, P.M.W. (2021) Ethnography and Medicine: The Utility of Positivist Methods in Ethnographic Research, *Anthropology and Medicine*.

1   Introduction

Introducing the Declarative Mapping Sentence

Attempting to assess or, in some other way, understand human or non-human animals is fraught with difficulties and inaccuracies. This is in part due to the subject matter, *covert and overt behaviour*, which are infinitely varied, complex and frequently idiosyncratic. It is also due to the fact that we can never truly and precisely know why a sentient creature behaves as they do. These caveats are true of the reactions and understandings a person has towards women in science fiction movies and television programmes. Of course, we are able to ask people to respond to pre-determined questions that have a quantitative rating, for example, on a 1 to 5 rating scale. We could, for instance, ask "to what extent do you feel that women are positively represented in science fiction movies," to which individuals could supply a number from 1 (very poorly represented) to 5 (very well represented). Of course, there are many other rating scales that could have been used and different words and phrases employed in the questions designed to tap specific psychological reactions. However, such questions face many problems. For example, they are predetermined by the researcher and may not represent the actual reaction that any person watching a movie may be having. They also assume that the response scale has a similar meaning to all respondents and that the numbers that form the response have a comparable meaning to different respondents. As said earlier, all forms of attempting to understand other people have these and other difficulties. However, with the use of numbers as a response and the standardised question employed, such a quantitative approach gives the potentially spurious impression of being authoritative and an accurate indicator of human understanding.

With these shortcomings in mind, many researchers have turned to a qualitative approach in their efforts to understand behaviour. When employing these approaches, the researcher typically asks open-ended and non-guiding questions that allow participants to have an open field of responses at their

DOI: 10.4324/9781003138419-1

disposal: The participants make the choice of what their reaction will be, not the researcher. One of the consequences of this type of qualitative research is that comparing responses is even more problematic. However, in this form of research, the researcher is not attempting to produce a cumulative or aggregated numerical indicator of a sample of peoples' reactions. Rather, qualitative researchers accept these limitations and attempt to discover rich insight in relation to how a person experiences a film or a television programme.

It is the authors' assertion that it is particularly the case that research into a film and a television programme has a subject matter that recommends itself to qualitative forms of data gathering and analysis. This is due to the complex ways in which characters, situations and storylines are intertwined in richly multifaceted ways and are highly idiosyncratic. As a consequence, research that attempts to reveal insight into the roles of specific women in a film must be able to subtly illuminate this complex richness. Furthermore, the way a researcher attempts to understand individuals or groups of people is intimately related to the philosophical position and stance they take towards research[1] (Brinkmann, 2018).

Researchers such as Hackett and Hayre (2020), Rapport and Braithwaite (2020) and many others would argue that meaningful insight into an individual and their experiences can best be achieved using qualitative research approaches. Such a statement is at least in part due to the subject matter of personal lives and experiences often being related to personal issues, features of life that are socially taboo or which possess a stigma, etc. In these situations, individuals may be unwilling or unable to reveal such information when surveyed. Here, and indeed in many other aspects of a persons' life, a researcher may have to employ an approach that includes some forms of observational procedure along with openly talking, participating and sharing with those people they are interested in. Taking such an approach, they hope, will allow them to get to know their participants and to be trusted by them. Ultimately, it is believed that qualitative forms of research will yield data in which researchers may place their trust. With the particular strengths and appropriateness of qualitative research (data collection and analysis) in mind, the declarative mapping sentence method (Hackett, 2019a, 2020a; Hackett and Schwarzenbach, 2020) for designing, conducting and analysing qualitative research is proposed as an additional or alternative approach that may usefully be used by film and television researchers. Moreover, the approach is appropriate both for analysing the content of moving media and for profiling its characters.

However, not all forms of qualitative research are the same in terms of how data are treated. One form of qualitative research transforms qualitative data into some forms of numerical information (Boyatzis, 1998) and allows the researcher to form initial hypotheses about the subject of the research. In this book, we are, however, concerned with maintaining the rich insights that exist in the data by leaving its qualitative nature intact. On such an understanding, qualitative research data take the form of narratives that may be thematically coded (Boyatzis, 1998). Under this understanding of qualitative research, the coding of information (in this book, coding of information that is related to the roles of women in science fiction films) is not a procedure that is undertaken only at the start of the analysis, but instead it is active and ongoing during which theories are generated about the content of the data and the interrelationships of themes that are present. Coding is continuous, and in the initial coding, hypotheses are developed and polished, removed, added to, etc., throughout the entirety of the analytical process. For example, in our research, theories about women's roles will be reshaped and brought together in the light of our ever more sophisticated considerations of our data. Furthermore, researchers will produce memos about their reactions to the data and the theoretical categorial structural that the researcher has developed to aid their interpretations.[2]

Hackett (2014b, 2020a, 2021a, 2021b), Cowle and Hackett (2021), Hackett and Fisher (2019), Koval and Hackett (2016) and Lustig and Hackett (2020a, 2020b) developed the declarative mapping sentence method as an extension of the quantitative traditional mapping sentence into the realm of qualitative research and as a tool to be used during the immersive, non-numerically reductive qualitative approach mentioned earlier. Research based on the declarative mapping sentence has been used in a wide variety of substantive research areas, for example: the characteristics of clinical reasoning (Wihlborg et al., 2019); ethnographic health research (Hackett, 2020b, 2019b); the impact of Covid-19 on transport planning in Austria (Morshed, 2020); for use within a talk-therapy setting as a clinical tool (Hackett, 2019a); illuminating relationships between people, technologies and concepts in complex systems (Devine-Wright, 2020); the appreciation and understanding of fine art (Hackett, 2017a, 2017b, 2016a, 2013; Cowle, 2018); student experiences of their higher education and their lives (Shkoler et al., 2020; Schwarzenbach and Hackett, 2015; Hackett, 2014a); visual impairment (Cowle, 2018; Hackett, 2013); religious experiences (Przybylska, 2014); bird behaviour (Hackett, 2019c); the classification of Cetacea (Guttman, 1985); Philosophy (Hackett, 2018, 2016b; Lustig and Hackett, 2020a, 2020b); racial discrimination (Hackett and Schwarzenbach, 2010); using information technology (Zhang et al., 2016).

The Critical Declarative Mapping Sentence

In our review of films and television productions, it seems obvious to state that the society within which these media were made and consumed will have a profound effect upon their content. It is equally true that the situations in which we, the two author/researchers, are located will have a great impact upon our evaluations of the films and television programmes. This being the case, we are interested in the social structures that influence, enable, constrain and, in other ways, influence experiences. Thus, we will assume a *critical* perspective in our research which will impact upon our interpretations of the media and how we report this (Terry and Hayfield, 2021) as "critical researchers engage in inquiry to promote liberation, transformation, consciousness raising, and social change" (Levitt, 2021). This point is also stressed by Fine and Torre (2021) who note that taking a critical perspective intentionally causes the researcher to focus on questions regarding power, injustice and intersectionality.

Levitt et al. (2017) defined two types of research that may be conducted within a critical paradigm. We will be adopting one of these specific types of the critical research approach in our investigation which will be a theory-driven approach in which the critical theory is used as a lens to guide our inquiries and analyses. Adopting a critical paradigm impels the researcher to examine the structures that exist in a society, the embedded power relationships and the roles of these in the promotion of social inequalities and the disenabling of people (Reimer-Kirkham et al., 2009). Thus, critical social research that is concerned with enabling social change (such as our research is concerned with the provision of more positive female in science fiction media) is part of the critical paradigm (Reid et al., 2017).

More specifically, we will be performing a thematic analysis of the visual media we observe which will take the specific form of critical thematic analysis (see, for example, Clarke and Braun, 2014; Clarke et al., 2015). We recognise that we are not neutral in our aims. Instead we are engaging in our enquiries and with aims that, according to Levitt (2021), are typical of the critical researcher, as we wish empower women: "to promote liberation, transformation, consciousness raising, and social change" (Levitt, 2021, p. 12).

Using the Declarative Mapping Sentence Method

In order to acquaint the reader with the qualities of the declarative mapping sentence method, it is useful to describe how the method is used and then to expand upon its properties. It should be noted that the method starts at the point in a research project where the researcher is generating his or her ideas that will form and underpin the study. The declarative mapping sentence method then continues to be influential at all stages of the research process including the design of a research procedure, the development of research tools, analysis, interpretation of findings and the suggestion of the meaning of results and propositions of future research.

When using the declarative mapping sentence method to analyse films and their characters, this approach can be understood in reference to the eight stages that a research goes through.[3]

Stage 1

The initial stage is made up of what are frequently rather poorly formed thoughts held by the researcher about the film or television programme they are interested in or the characters in these. The researcher then reflects upon these thoughts and integrates and organises these in reference to their experiences and the existing literature that impacts upon the area of research interest. During this time, the researcher is taking down his or her impressions about what are believed to be the most pertinent features of the film and/or its characters. When using the declarative mapping sentence method, the pertinent features in any research domain are termed as facets, and sub-aspects of these are called elements and the researcher attempts to identify these in reference to the film and the research questions.

Stage 2

The researcher then takes the notes and memos that they developed in stage 1 and refines these into a sub-set of features (facets). The researcher also attempts to identify sub-aspects of the facets (pertinent features of the film and characters) that have been identified. These sub-categories are called facet elements.

Stage 3

During stage 3, the researcher writes an initial declarative mapping sentence within which the facets and elements identified in the previous stage are incorporated into the sentence. A declarative mapping sentence is a sentence written in normal English prose. Words and phrases are tentatively chosen to connect the facets that reflect the hypothesised relationship between the facets and their elements in reference to the film or character of interest. It should be kept in mind that it is very likely that this initial declarative statement will be significantly altered as the research design progresses.

Stage 4

This next stage embodies a process that is repeated throughout the use of the declarative mapping sentence method and involves the researcher in standing back from the research process and reflecting upon the declarative mapping sentence he or she has produced in relation to the films and characters that are the focus of the research. If necessary, the researcher modifies the sentence in terms of its facets, their elements and the way their interrelationships are suggested through the use of connecting words and phrases. It is important that these modifications are only undertaken due to the empirical relationships as they appear in the film and characters being studied.

Stage 5

When conducting primary research, a researcher using a declarative mapping sentence method has to design their data gathering approach and tools based upon the declarative mapping sentence. Questions, observations, analysis templates, coding schedules, focus groups' interview schedules, indepth interviews, digital ethnographies, etc., are produced using the structural hypotheses present in the study's declarative mapping sentence. That is, instruments are developed that incorporate the facets and elements of the declarative mapping sentence organised in such a manner as suggested by the sentence and its connective phrases. Data are then gathered using the instruments that have been so designed.[4]

Stage 6

During the sixth stage in the declarative mapping sentence method, the analysis of data is commenced.

At **stage 6A**, the researcher considers and compares features, events, incidents, etc., in the data that are germane to the description offered by the facets and elements in the sentence and seeks to illustrate and illuminate, add, delete or modify these declarative components, as they relate to the film or character being considered.

Stage 6B involves attempting to confidently bring together the facets and elements in a way that provides a greater understanding of how the facets interact in the understandings of those who are analysing the film or its characters. This is a repetition of stage 4 and results in the modification of the initial declarative mapping sentence stated in stage 3. In essence, the declarative mapping sentence method is a process of honing of the sentence in relation to the data. This process results in the stating of a modified declaration of the pertinent components of an analysis in a declarative mapping sentence format.

During the processes involved in the aforementioned stages, and especially in stages 6A and 6B, the researcher codes events, incidents, states of affairs, etc., in a film using the facets and elements present in the sentence and repeatedly compares and contrasts a current event or incident in the data with those coded earlier. By doing this, modifications of the sentence are suggested and these are noted. Comparing how different filmic events and aspects of a character have been coded using the sentence's facets and elements suggests both the bounds and the theoretical nature of the facets and elements, and these may be modified accordingly. The more data that are coded, the more fully the researcher comes to appreciate the ways in which the facets exist within the context of the film and its characters and when and where the facets are particularly important, irrelevant, consequential, etc. The researcher also becomes aware of how these facets and elements interact with the other facets and elements that are in the declarative sentence.

At all points in the analysis process, the researcher is encouraged to keep memos about the ideas that come in to their mind regarding the coding process and the structure of the sentence they are working with. It is imperative that the insights that a researcher has when working with a declarative mapping sentence to code data related to a film or a character are recorded at the time of the analysis. This is of particular significance so as to allow sensitive and skilful insights that may be revealed during the analysis to be incorporated into the studies of the declarative mapping sentence. It is also important that the analysis process is not rushed and that the researcher has the time to reflect methodically and systematically on the relationship between the data and the structure of the sentence in terms of its facets and elements and the ways in which these are connected together. The importance of this process cannot be overemphasised, as it is to be remembered that the declarative mapping sentence not only attempts to provide an account for the pertinent aspects of a research domain but it also offers a plausible suggestion as to how these categorial aspects come together in a way that provides insight into a film or a character.[5]

Stage 7

Stage 7 involves using the declarative sentence developed in stage 5 to frame writing about the research that has been undertaken, and the mapping sentence's components (the facets and the elements) are used to structure the presentation of a researcher's findings and to offer details about how the data have been analysed. This stage also requires a researcher to reflect upon and justify their results and to proffer illustrations from their data to bring credibility to their interpretations.

Stage 8

The final stage requires the researcher to overtly delimit the extent of their findings and the bounds of the theoretical statements contained within their declarative mapping sentence. This means that the mapping sentence is named so as to make clear the films and characters that are being described. For example, it should be clearly stated whether the mapping sentence describes a specific character, a type of character, a film or a genre of films.

It should be noted that the eight stages I have presented serve to illustrate the process of using a declarative mapping sentence when analysing a film or a film character. However, the numbering of the stages suggests a rigid sequential procedure that is often not how the method ends up being used as the researcher who employs a declarative mapping sentence continually revisits earlier stages of this process. It is also worthy of note that the declarative mapping sentence method may be used in team research projects to enable researchers to reflect upon points they may have missed or miscoded. In team research, it is also possible to compare how each team member has used the sentence to code a given film or character (data set) and to become aware of the similarities and differences between these codings.

Previously, I have suggested that when using a declarative mapping sentence, the process of repeatedly revisiting the original film, or data that have been derived from the film, during the whole of the analysis period is amalgamated by explicitly proposing an initial structure or hypothesised thematic categories that are believed to help our understanding of the film or the character. Therefore, the declarative mapping sentence utilises an explicit coding procedure along with continually going back and forth between data and analyses. This process in theory development in the qualitative analysis is commented upon by many authors including Divine-Wright (2020) and is one of the strengths of the use of declarative mapping sentences: Due to the fact that the original hypotheses in regards to data analysis are not rigidly held but are constantly tested and revised, they facilitate theory development by not imposing a pre-determined or a permanent coding schedule for a data set. The declarative mapping sentence method is also a systematic and thorough way of generating theories about the meaning of the data being analysed. Another benefit of the declarative mapping sentence method is that it does not impede the delicate and penetrating understanding that the researcher develops of their qualitative understanding of a film. Rather, when a researcher uses the declarative mapping sentence method, the approach aspires to draw out such sensitivities towards the film and its associated data and the production of theories based upon a developing understanding regarding its content. The use of the method places the researcher centrally in the analytic process, and its successful usage relies upon an empathetic understanding and the skill of the researcher.

In addition, the use of the method enables direct comparisons between the analyses of two or more researchers who are working on the same film or characters, while not implying that they will arrive at exactly the same result. The essence of the method is that it has a flexible and modifiable structure and that it also allows for imprecision and uniqueness in the generation of theories about the film-related data.

Another essential feature of the method that the theoretical structures embodied in a declarative mapping sentence may be readily transformed into research tools and procedures which cross-examine the proposed theoretical structures. It is important to note that the declarative mapping sentence method simultaneously addresses multiple hypotheses that are understood to structure or influence the data that have arisen from a film at what may not be a similar level of generality or specificity. However, the hypotheses are assumed to intermingle to constitute the domain of interest and to provide a limit to the area of interest within an explicit theoretical structure.

When using an analytic induction approach (Hammersley, 2004; Hammersley and Cooper, 2012; Znaniecki, 1934), a researcher also has the aim of producing an integrated account of a research domain but aims for precise and generalisable causal theories. The declarative mapping sentence method has different aims and adopts a different approach to analytic induction which results in plausible and justifiable propositions regarding the theoretical structure and content of the domain being investigated. It is unlikely that a piece of research designed using the declarative mapping sentence method will result in the discovery of causal associations. Instead, a depiction of circumstances, situations, effects, dimensions, sorts, types, categories and sub-categories, processes, etc., will more probably be the outcome. Any format of qualitative data associated with film or television that arises from observations, interviews, ethnography, projective techniques, netnography, textual narratives, auto-ethnography, etc., gathered in person or online, may be included in a declarative mapping sentence method study. Declarative mapping sentence methods are also able to analyse different types of data within a single or multiple studies. In addition, different qualitative methodologies and their arising data may be analysed together when using the methodology.

Throughout a research project, it is worth noting that the researcher continually revisits and re-considers facets and elements in relation to the declarative mapping sentence as a whole and reflects upon these in relation to the empirical nature of the film or character being studied. Reflection commences in relation to the researcher's own experiences and the literature from which the study's declarative mapping sentence was built. Once data are being scrutinised in analyses, notes, memos, etc., this reflective feedback allows modification of the sentence's facets, elements and the words and phrases that connect these.

To illustrate this process, if we take, as an example, a piece of research that is interested in understanding how a person with disabilities is portrayed in a movie, a very simple initial declarative mapping for this content is as follows.

The example in Figure 1.1 is an extremely simplified illustration of a declarative mapping sentence. In reality, it is likely that there would be more facets and facet elements along with highly detailed connective phraseology. The simplicity of this example, however, allows a greater understanding of a declarative mapping sentence. In this initial declarative mapping sentence, the researcher reflects upon his or her experiences of the movie portrayal of people with disabilities and their familiarity with how this has been written and commented about by other researchers interested in this topic.

The mapping sentence has three facets or major characteristics of how people with disabilities are portrayed in films: disability type; other

Person (x) who is a person with:

Disability type

– *physical*
– *mental*
– *both*

disabilities, where their disabilities are:

Other health issues

– *impacted by other health issues*
– *not impacted by other health issues*

is portrayed as living:

Living circumstances

– *independently*
– *with home visits*
– *in a care home*

Legend: emboldened = facet names; italics = facet elements

Figure 1.1 Initial Declarative Mapping Sentence for Understanding the Portrayal of a Person With Disabilities in a Film

health issues; living circumstances. From preliminary inspection of the literature and their own experiences, the researchers were able to divide each of the facets to reflect qualities of each of the facets as follows: disability type (physical, mental, both physical and mental); other health issues (impacted by other health issues, not impacted by other health issues); and living circumstances (independently, with home visits, in a care home). The three facets were then joined together using phrases that suggested the manner in which the facets were initially believed to relate to each other within the context of the portrayal of individuals with disabilities in films.

The declarative mapping sentence method achieves its aim of capturing the entirety of the experiential representation of people in films and television by reading through the mapping sentence several times. On each of these readings, the facet name is not read but rather a different facet element is read in its place. Readings are repeated changing the permutation of elements within the sentence. For example, one reading is:

Person (x) who is a person with a physical disability, where their disabilities are impacted by other health issues, is portrayed as living independently.

On this reading, the person has both physical and other disabilities, but they are shown as living independently. An alternative reading would be:

Person (x) who is a person with both physical and mental disabilities, where their disabilities are not impacted by other health issues is portrayed as living in a care home.

The use of the initial declarative mapping sentence enables the researcher to have a framework within which they attempt to understand their observation of the disabled person in the film. It should be noted that the scene or film may be classified using the mapping sentence or individual characters may be assigned a profile that demonstrates how the character is individually depicted. The initial declarative sentence framework may be used to design a frame to enable observations of people with disabilities in movies to be coded, and when this approach is used with several different movies, or characters in movie(s), it may become obvious that the facets, elements and connective parts of the sentence need to be modified.

For example, inspection of the data that came out of analysis of movies suggested that the characters with disabilities were portrayed differentially in terms of their mobility. This led to the inclusion of a facet of mobility in Figure 1.2.

Person (x) who is a person with:

Disability type
- *physical*
- *mental*
- *both*

disabilities, where their disabilities are:

Other health issues
- *impacted by other health issues*
- *not impacted by other health issues*

is portrayed as living:

Living circumstances
- *independently*
- *with home visits*
- *in a care home*

and were shown to be:

Mobility
- *independently mobile*
- *dependent upon others for mobility*
- *largely immobile*

Legend: emboldened = facet names; italics = facet elements

Figure 1.2 Modified Declarative Mapping Sentence for Understanding the Portrayal of a Person With Disabilities in a Film

An example of a reading from this modified declarative mapping sentence could be:

> Person (x) who is a person with both physical and mental disabilities, where their disabilities are impacted by other health issues is portrayed as living in a care home and being dependent upon others for mobility.

As well as enabling the coding of movie representations of disabled characters, the declarative mapping sentence method makes it possible to clearly specify and to draw bounds around the scope of the research study into movie representations of disability.

However, the flexibility of the approach enables further development of the sentence as a result of further experience using its framework to code movies. In this instance, after watching movies, it was felt that a new facet of movie type could usefully be included as a background facet. A background facet embodies any aspect of the situation that is being scrutinised but which is not a direct part of the content of interest. An example may clarify this. Watching and coding suggested that whether the film was directly about disability and that it placed disability centrally within its narrative or whether disability was peripherally located, or even largely unimportant to the film's narrative could impact upon the ways in which disabled individuals were portrayed. That is, the elements of this background facet enabled a greater understanding of the content of the movie. Therefore, the mapping sentence was further modified to incorporate this background facet and is shown in Figure 1.3.

The inclusion of this background facet within the declarative mapping sentence enables a refined understanding of portrayal of people with disabilities within film and television. The adapted declarative mapping sentence also allows for the evaluation of character's stories about aspects of their disability, for instance, their loss of mobility, which may be related to the other facets (e.g. their living circumstances and their other health conditions), and the mapping sentence suggested a framework for the holistic experience of disability by characters. In this way, the originally hypothesised facets are integrated with other facets that emerged during the research process. By using the declarative mapping sentence method with different movies or characters, it is possible to develop further a theory for the ways in which disability is portrayed and to enable suggestions to be made in regards to positive and negative aspects of these depictions.

As I have already noted, as well as providing an account of the content of a domain of interest, the declarative mapping sentence places boundaries around a research domain. That is, as well as declaring the pertinent aspects of a research domain, it states what is not within the mapping sentence as not being part of the particular study. This boundary of exclusion is also flexible and is likely to move in response to the data that are gathered. For example, mobility was initially not considered as part of the domain of the aforementioned research project, but its inclusion became essential in order to understand the data that had been gathered. Thus, the declarative mapping sentence method mitigates against the inclusion of what could be irrelevant

Person (x) who is in a film in which:

Centrality of disability
- *disability is placed centrality in its narrative*
- *disability is placed peripherally in its narrative*
- *disability is largely unimportant to its narrative*

is a person with:

Disability type
- *physical*
- *mental*
- *both*

disabilities, where their disabilities are:

Other health issues
- *impacted by other health issues*
- *not impacted by other health issues*

is portrayed as living:

Living circumstances
- *independently*
- *with home visits*
- *in a care home*

and were shown to be:

Mobility
- *independently mobile*
- *dependent upon others for mobility*
- *largely immobile*

Legend: emboldened = facet names; italics = facet elements

Figure 1.3 Modified Declarative Mapping Sentence for Understanding the Portrayal of a Person With Disabilities in a Film Including Background Facet

and overwhelming data while not being so rigid that it is not responsive to the evidence that is gathered. As more research with a declarative mapping sentence's framework is conducted, the sentence's theoretical structure hardens and becomes more trustworthy as large modifications of the sentence become fewer. Modifications of the sentence do continue to occur, but these tend to become in terms of the addition, deletion or modifications of facet elements and the words or phrases used to connect facets rather than the facets themselves. Such alterations are made to achieve a more logical structure to the sentence or to more clearly, parsimoniously and accurately define the nature of the movie or character under investigation. The connective phraseology in particular is subject to modification so as to better suggest the lived experience of the facets in the sentence. Elements may also be reduced in their number, as overlap and redundancy may become apparent.

Through the thorough and sometimes exhaustive inclusion and exclusion of facets and their elements in a declarative mapping sentence, the sentence becomes a theory of the structure of a specific aspect of films and television. By undertaking further refinement, it is also possible that the theory in the sentence may be modified to be appropriate for other similar areas of research. In the present example, through careful and reflective consideration and later data collection, the declarative mapping sentence for understanding the portrayal of disability in film may be extended so as to be appropriate to other types of health and illness portrayal in movies. It should be noted here that the generalisable aspects of the sentence are likely to be the content facets and the connective phraseology. The facet elements and the background facets are more likely to be specific to a given film or television programme. It is by stating an initial declarative mapping sentence and then using in the analysis of different types of media content that confidence in the structure of a declarative mapping sentence may be strengthened.

It is also the case that as a specific declarative mapping sentence is used in multiple studies and with a greater body of research data, the process of data analysis becomes more focused. The researcher develops an understanding of the qualitative data he or she is working with and coding and is able to delimit the facets and facet elements into which he or she is coding in accordance with the mapping sentence, and more detailed and refined appreciation of the data becomes possible. The researcher is therefore able to apply more energy to the exact nature of the facets present in an analysis. It also becomes obvious that the facets and their elements are eventually theoretically full or complete. The repeated use of a declarative mapping sentence to code data will suggest that when a movie or television programme has been coded on multiple occasions into a given facet, it is relatively easy to identify when a new or novel aspect of the phenomena can be coded in this way or if a modification of the facet is needed in terms of element adaptation.

A declarative mapping sentence is a collection of independent facets of personal experience that are comprised of sub-elements that are themselves independent aspects of the facet's content. The elements of a facet are increased in number or sub-divided until they become saturated, and new data can be coded without the addition of a new element. The process of adding, modifying and deleting facets and their elements is central to any project in which the declarative mapping sentence is employed. Indeed, in such research, the statement of an initial declarative mapping sentence is the theoretical start of the research which continues through a series of modifications to the sentence and ends in the statement of the refined sentence as an empirically upheld statement of the research content.

A declarative mapping sentence is a theoretical delimitation of a research content in terms of the facets and elements used to describe it. Confidence is established in the declarative mapping sentence through the saturation of its categories by the data collected. If necessary, more data are collected in order to extend the theoretical limits of the sentence. However, this is a frugal exercise, as the data gathered are analysed within the structural qualities of the declarative mapping sentence, which allows the paring down of large amounts of qualitative information. This mitigates against the problem that may come about when dealing with large amounts of data themes and categories can become almost arbitrary. In this situation this may not lead to the establishment of consistent understanding of a research area.

The declarative mapping sentence methodology also offers a structure that may be incorporated when writing a report or preparing a presentation about the study. In order to write within and about a facet's content, it is necessary to assemble the notes and transcripts that have been coded within specific facets and to further sub-divide these into facet elements. This is a less onerous task than may be expected, as the facets were initially used to design the research, and assembling of data to summarise in this way may suggest further analysis and insights. Once the data have been assembled in this way, it may be accessed to allow verbatim illustrations to be used.

When using a declarative mapping sentence method to structure the presentation of the results of a project, the facets and their elements form the sections into which analysis and writing are broken down. For example, the mapping sentence in Figure 1.3 offers a template that may consider the centrality of the disability in terms of how centrally within the films narrative disability is placed. As this is a background facet, care would be taken to relate this to the understanding that is developed from the other (content) facets. Another section would be about the type of disability the character is shown as having with this being sub-divided into physical disabilities, mental disabilities or a combination of these. Other health issues would also be considered, as these impacted upon the portrayal of the character with disability. Sections would also be developed that considered the independence a character had in terms of mobility and separately in terms of living. In these, the respective sub-sections would be about the degree to which the character was shown to be independently mobile, dependent upon others for mobility or largely immobile and the degree to which they were portrayed as living independently, with visits at home from health professionals or within some form of residential care setting.

In this way, the full richness of characters' stories would be presented within a framework that allowed for the emergence of the commonalities and differences in the portrayal of people with disabilities within films.

Summary of the Declarative Mapping Sentence Method

It is important that we start the conclusion to this section by stressing that:

> the declarative mapping sentence is a framework within which a discussion may be facilitated of the richly varied and infinitely complex differences and similarities in behaviour as these relate to a specific topic of interest.

This is particularly central to understanding the use of the declarative mapping sentence method, as it emphasises the qualitative and interpretative nature of this research process and the form of the outcomes from this type of research.

Another aspect of the method that needs to be mentioned is that elements themselves may be sub-divided to have sub-elements. This was not mentioned during the initial description of the declarative mapping sentence so as not to confuse those new to the approach and also because elements are not typically sub-divided. However, an example of a facet with elements that may be sub-divided is that of the disability type facet that is present in the aforementioned three figures (Figures 1.1–1.3). In this facet, the structure may be modified through the inclusion of sub-elements, thus:

Disability type

- *Physical*

    - *deteriorating*
    - *stable*
    - *improving*

- *Mental*

    - *deteriorating*
    - *stable*
    - *improving*

- *Both*

  - *deteriorating*
  - *stable*
  - *improving*

In this example, I have included the same three sub-elements for the three elements of the facet. However, this may not always be the case, and a single element alone may have sub-elements and/or the elements may have different sub-elements.

When using the declarative mapping sentence method, the characteristics of the movies or television programmes being studied are specified in a coherent and logical theory of content that is present in the facets, elements, connective ontology and in the declarative mapping sentence as a whole. It should be noted that the method may be used as either an exploratory or a confirmatory approach. The declarative mapping sentence is used exploratively in order to examine a research domain that has not previously been investigated using this approach so as to develop a coherent thematic structure that accounts for variation in the qualitative data. In this situation, the researcher may bring a tentative understanding of the research area's content with him or her to the analysis situation which has come from their previous experience or findings in related qualitative literature on similar research content. The researcher may also come to the analysis with a relatively open mind and may allow the data itself to almost completely guide their coding. When the research is confirmatory, the research area will have previously been investigated using the declarative mapping sentence method; the declarative mapping sentence that arose from the findings of the previous research will be used to guide research design, coding and the interpretation of the new content area. The existing sentence will then be confirmed, refuted and/or modified in reference to the new area it has been applied to. The declarative mapping sentence method also offers a consistent approach for undertaking longitudinal research which provides a framework within which changes in patients' responses over time are understood.

Glaser (1965, p. 443) notes, "a perennial problem with qualitative analysis is conveying the credibility" of the analysis that has been performed. This difficulty may be addressed by showing how an analysis developed its results by presenting data to support the conclusions drawn. However, when an analysis and its findings are complex, offering data to illustrate findings may result in a document that is difficult to read. When a researcher is using the declarative mapping sentence method to qualitatively investigate film or television, their research conclusions are readily expressed in the form of the theoretical declarations that the mapping sentence embodies in terms of its facetted structure. This structure for the content of the media that is being interrogated is stated prior to the commencement of data collection and is referred to throughout the entire research process. The coding of data and the explanations regarding the final thematic structure of an analysis are constant, and the reader of the research findings is not struggling to understand how the coding came about or how conclusions about the film, programme or character were reached. The pursuance of analysis within an explicitly stated framework also mitigates against the feeling that the reader may have that analysis of the qualitative data in a research project is a somewhat imprecise and impressionistic reaction to the film's content.

It is important, however, that analysis is undertaken sensitively and the data that arise from a movie are not forced to fit within the mapping sentence's structure. The authors have not found this to be a problem, as pressure is not placed upon a researcher to stick to the initially stated structure and equal gravity is accorded to findings whether these are in the form of a declarative mapping sentence's structure that is the same as its initial form or modified to a smaller or greater extent. The declarative mapping sentence method requires the researcher to continually revisit the data from the film that is being coded and to attempt to make sense of both the data and the sentence's structure, which aids in understanding the facets and elements along with their interrelationships. By undertaking such an open and declared process, the credibility of interpretations in relation to a film is enhanced.

The declarative mapping sentence forms a complex structural hypothesis of the data that are being analysed. Repeated applications of the sentence to different data sets allow consideration of the patterns of similarity and difference present in the data, for confidence to grow in the interpretations that the sentence proclaims in its structure and for theory to be developed in regards to the research content. As the sentence is transferrable to different research contexts, subsequent analyses uphold or modify the structure and also provide further insight into the changing relationships between the facets and their elements. For example, as a researcher gathers more information about the portrayal of individuals with disabilities, his or her understanding of the extent to which the portrayal of loss of mobility may change and how these changes may alter our understanding about disabled people and their life issues. The declarative mapping sentence method, through its constant though flexible format, is sensitive to the exploration of such dynamic situations.

The declarative mapping sentence represents ideas and themes that are more general than the specific data that are being analysed. This is due to the fact that the facets and elements represent qualities around which underlying similarities and differences in the data gathered may vary. When a declarative mapping methodology is used to analyse a substantive area that is new to scrutiny through the method, as is our case with the role of women in science fiction movies and television programmes, what arises from analysis is a theory of the structure for this area.

However, if the declarative mapping sentence method is subsequently used to look at women's roles in science fiction, the existing declarative mapping sentence that we develop for our research may be used to design the new research. In this situation, the researcher is engaging in expanding the sentence's extent of generality from a specific case to the process of formal theory development for the conceptual area of women's roles in science fiction. Furthermore, the method allows for the development of understanding of the content of a declarative mapping sentence (facets and elements) in relation to specific contexts, and it also facilitates propositions based upon the sentence and its facets and elements.[6]

Having taken some time to set the scene in terms of the methodology of our research, we now turn to the substantive content of our subject matter that being women's portrayal in science fiction.

Developing Declarative Mapping Sentences for Understanding the Portrayal of Women in Science Fiction Films

As we are concerned in the evaluation of the role of women in science fiction moving media, it is worthy of note that defining the genre of science fiction itself is not a simple matter (Johnston, 2011). In fact, Johnston sees science fiction as drawing from a wide and diverse set of ideas or similarities and where the genre is constantly changing and that it is in fact, "a volatile contemporary discourse" (Johnston, 2011, p. 25). With this in mind, we will adopt the approach of such writers such as Penley et al. (1991) and Rickman (2004) and assume that people reading this book have somewhat of an understanding of science fiction as a genre and we will concentrate upon female representations in four specific aspects of films from this genre: This is of course not to dismiss the complex interplay that exists between film and the broader historical and cultural context. The role and power that women are portrayed as having have been an important element within the future worlds that have been created in science fiction films. Several of these gazes into the future have been provided by American films which have often posited the notion that a future world would be run by women. This is especially true of films from the early twentieth century and reflected the increased roles and power of women in society. In these films, men come to the rescue in a mismanaged female run world. However, as Johnston (2011) suggests, the link between society and the understanding of a film is to accept that the fantasy created bares elements of the contemporary but to recognise that the films draw upon multiple influences and is not a simple reflection of a culture's anxieties.

The world has changed in the 55 years since the first television episode of Star Trek was aired, and women are now central in many science films and television programmes. Similarly, women's role in science fiction films has changed, as they have increasingly portrayed individuals in power in what is often seen as a genre that is produced by men for men. Throughout much of the history of science fiction films, women have tended to be cast in secondary or supportive roles to their male counterparts. This appears to be related to the historical epoch and culture within which films from this genre have been made.[7] As the current book is mainly methodological rather than being a book primarily concerned with a film or a gender, we consider the roles of women in movie media to the extent that our consideration illustrates how we developed and used the declarative mapping sentence method in order to illustrate the roles of women characters in this genre.

The Choice of Television Programmes and Films

We have included a mere four pieces of science fiction media in our research: two television programmes and two films. Having a small sample of media, we decided to choose examples of films and programmes that provided examples of engaging and progressive gender representations and, or, were productions that were seen as noteworthy. For example, we chose Star Trek, as it has been claimed that the series embodied a utopian vision, "it pushed the limits of diversity, progressivism and inclusion on television and the science fiction genre" (Olla, 2021). Olla was writing on the occasion of the actor William Shatner, who played the lead role in Star Trek as captain of the Starship Enterprise and was going into space in a privately owned and for-profit space vehicle. Olla continues to note that Star Trek had its foundations in utopian 1960s' notions which pushed the usual standards of diversity and inclusiveness in the media and especially in science fiction. Of particular relevance to the present book, it has also been claimed that Star Trek played a seminal role in the advancement of the roles played and the depiction of women and people of colour. For these reasons, we decided to include the television programmes in our sample.

It is perhaps worth taking a moment to reflect on William Shatner's space ride. Olla (2021) claims that he is making a mistake in taking this trip to the edge of space and allying himself with the Owner of the Blue Origin spaceship company, Jeff Bazos. Olla continues to note how Bazos' enterprise embodies a retrograde step from the characters of Star Trek and the show's attempts to portray a utopian picture of humankind. We agree with this author that the worlds of Bazos and Star Trek are antithetical and that Shatner's actions are adversarial to notions of inclusivity and that rather his actions reflect the deeply embodied association between, as Olla puts it, capitalism and colonialism to not pollute the inclusive aims of Star Trek. Indeed, Bazos' Blue Origin is in competition with Elon Musk's company SpaceX according to Olla, and comes out of the worst of capitalism and represents a colonial act. This is very different to the utopian world of Star Trek in which poverty and capitalism have both been eliminated, even though colonialism is still embraced. Olla (2021) concludes that there is much to praise in Star Trek, such as a very early interracial kiss but that more recent Star Trek productions have been hindered by a desire to sell the franchise as widely as possible and have led to women being relegated to silent supports to male-based action scenes.

Using the Declarative Mapping Sentence to Analyse Selected Films and Television Shows

The broad subject matter of this research is the consideration of the portrayal of characters in film and television. However, after reviewing the literature, the authors were unable to discover research into this area that employed a mapping sentence. Therefore, the research was exploratory and our first task was to develop an initial declarative mapping sentence for the area. As demonstrated in the examples given earlier in this chapter, the development of a mapping sentence is usually not something that happens at a single moment, where the researcher sits down and writes his or her completed and finalised mapping sentence. This was most certainly not the case in this research in which our declarative mapping sentence progressed through many iterations. Prior to stating any form of mapping sentence, we viewed relevant movies and read literature on both science fiction films and female roles in movies in an attempt to identify the main dimensions along which women's roles could be understood. We then noted what we considered to be pertinent facets and their elements and discussed these. After this, we wrestled with the aspects of women's representation that we should include and the precise form of the aspects we included. A very obvious example we felt was whether the main woman or women in a film occupied lead or supportive roles. We decided to include this as a facet in our first mapping sentence and we chose the elements of lead and support. In addition to this facet, in total, we stated four facets with their respective elements. The facets, along with their elements in parentheses, are as follows:

Facets (elements)

Role (lead, support);
Femme Fatale (femme fatale, not a femme fatale);
Strength (in power, responds to male power);
Gaze (male, female, neutral, other).

The four facets and their respective elements were combined within a sentence format that reflected what we believed to be the empirical interrelationships between the facets. This resulted in the first declarative mapping sentence for classifying science fiction films and television in terms of their portrayal of women and that took the following format.

This four-facet declarative mapping sentence (in Figure 1.4) was rudimentary, but it served as a platform for further consideration of the roles of the women in the films we were reviewing. Independently, the two authors looked at the four films and considered the roles of the women in these in terms of the facets and elements in the mapping sentence. This resulted in us discussing our use of the facets and their elements in characterising the women. We discovered that many of the elements did not articulate the

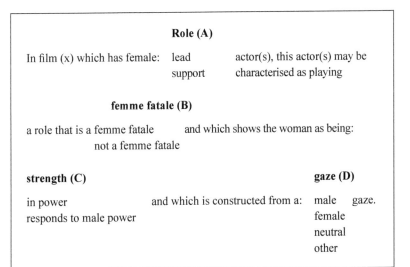

Figure 1.4 First Mapping Sentence for Women in Science Fiction

	Role (A)		looks (B)
In the film (x) which has a female:	lead: support	actor (s), who:	emphasises does not emphasise

		femme fatale (C)
her looks, where this woman may be characterised as playing a role that is a:		femme fatale not a femme fatale

	physical strength (D)	
and which shows the woman as being physically:	strong neutral weak	and as being:

emotional strength (E)		gaze (F)	
independent reliant upon men	and which is constructed from a:	male female neutral other	gaze.

Figure 1.5 Second Mapping Sentence for Women in Science Fiction

characteristics we intended or were redundant, and we found that new facets and new elements for existing facets were needed. Through these discussions, we changed the mapping sentence many times until we arrived at the following facets and elements and a revised mapping sentence (Figure 1.5) and that took the following format:

Facets (elements)

> Role (lead, support);
> Looks (emphasises, does not);
> Femme Fatale (femme fatale, not a femme fatale);
> Physical Strength (strong, neutral, weak);

Emotional Strength (independent, reliant upon men);
Gaze (male, female, neutral, other).

Over the next few days, we then watched the selected movies and other science fiction films and television programmes with the explicit intent of attempting to see to what extent the mapping sentence provided a framework for understanding the roles of the women in the media we viewed. Again, this led to a prolonged discussion between us about the mapping sentence and how it needed to be modified. This then led to another series of changes in the facets (elements) and the mapping sentence (Figure 1.6) and resulted in the following.

Facets (elements)

Role (central, peripheral, not emphasised);
Sexual Appearance (overly emphasised, moderately emphasised);
Bad Woman (femme fatale, bad in other ways, not bad);
Physical Strength (strong, neutral, weak);
Personal Authority (independent, dependent, neutral);
Position to Others (collaborates with other, relies on men, challenges others);
Gaze (male, female, neutral, other).

As can be seen, the changes we made included the addition of several facets and their elements. However, after further discussion, it was felt that facets E and F overlapped and did not clearly embody what was important in differentiating the roles of female characters in science fiction films. We therefore merged and slightly altered these two facets to form a new facet E – Personal Authority. The facets and elements were thus modified:

Facets (elements)

Role (central, peripheral);
Sexual Appearance (overly emphasises, moderately emphasised, not emphasised);
Bad Woman (femme fatale, bad in other ways, not bad);
Physical Strength (strong, neutral, weak);
Personal Authority (independent, dependent, neutral);

role (A)	sexual appearance (B)
In the film (x) which has a female actor(s) with a :	central, role, who: peripheral not emphasised	overly emphasised moderately emphasised

	bad woman (C)
her sexual appearance, where this role may be characterised as playing a part that is a:	femme fatale bad in other way not bad

	physical strength (D)	
and which shows the woman as being physically:	strong neutral weak	and as being:

personal authority (E)		position to others (F)
independent dependent neutral	and who is in a position in which she:	collaborates with others, relies on men challenges others

	gaze (G)	
and is constructed to satisfy the:	male female neutral other	gaze.

Figure 1.6 Third Mapping Sentence for Women in Science Fiction

Gaze (male, female, neutral, other).

The resulting mapping sentence (Figure 1.7) then took the following form:

However, after further discussion, we decided that the declarative mapping sentence needed further modification, and through both independent and combined discussion, we decided to remove the facet of gaze and we arrived at facets, elements and the finalised mapping sentence shown in Figure 1.8.

role (A)	sexual appearance (B)
In the film (x) which has a central, role, who: female actor(s) with a : peripheral	overly emphasised moderately emphasised not emphasised

bad woman (C)

her sexual appearance, where this role may be   femme fatale
characterised as playing a part that is a: bad in other way
                                                                              not bad

physical strength (D)

and which shows the woman   strong   and as being in an:
as being physically: neutral
                                               weak

personal authority (E)

independent   position relative to others, and is
dependent   constructed to satisfy the:
neutral

gaze (F)

male   gaze.
female
neutral
other

Figure 1.7 Fourth Mapping Sentence for Women in Science Fiction

Facets (elements)

> Role (lead role, support role);
> Sexual Appearance (not emphasises, moderately emphasised, overly emphasised);
> Bad Woman (not bad, bad in other ways, femme fatale);

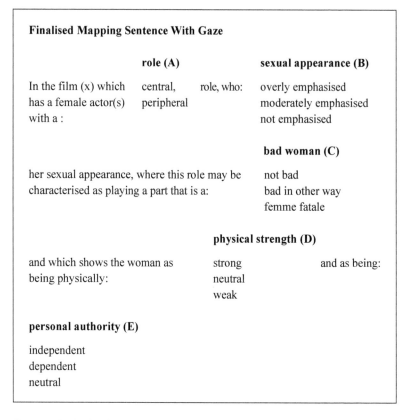

Figure 1.8 Finalised Mapping Sentence for Women in Science Fiction

Physical Strength (strong, neutral, weak);
Personal Authority (fully independent, partly independent and partly dependent, fully dependent).

It is apparent from our account of the aforementioned developmental process that the origination of a declarative mapping sentence facilitates thought, reflection and discussion. This is one of the strengths of adopting the approach. Furthermore, while the finalised mapping sentence shown earlier is the one we took into our analyses, this may not be the mapping sentence we are satisfied with at the end of our research.

Conclusions

In this chapter, we have introduced the genre of science fiction film and television and the portrayal of women in these productions as the area of our research. We have not gone into depths upon this genre of film, as the book is largely methodological. For this reason, we have spent considerable time introducing the declarative mapping sentence methodology as the approach we will use to analyse our research. We described the approach and went through in detail how to use a declarative mapping sentence to analyse a film and provided examples of how to do this. Finally, we took the reader through the stages we went through in developing the declarative mapping sentence for our research. In the next chapter, we turn to our initial analysis which is of the first ever episode of the first Star Trek television series.

Notes

1. This is true both within the context of film and television and in any other aspect of human life.
2. There is an underlying dialog that is occurring when we use words in qualitative research. This involves a variety of contrasts that is much broader than the declarative mapping sentence method. It involves, according to Crystal (2017) a series of contrasts, "between words and things, words and deeds, words and thoughts, words and ideas" (p. 24). Crystal continues to note that these pairings have been the source of much scholarship which has resulted in words being seen as, "inadequate representations of thoughts, poor replacements for actions, or a dangerous distraction from experiential realities . . . (or alternately as) . . . indispensable for the expression of thoughts , a valuable alternative to actions, or a means of finding order in inchoate realities" (p. 24). Qualitative health research therefore, as it deals largely with words as expressions of patients, may be seen as inadequate representations of thoughts, actions, etc. Mapping sentences are similarly bound. However, as Malinowski (1935) said, words are a component of action and are action's equivalents, and while not entirely endorsing this position they are perhaps the best information source that we possess regarding the internal states of patients in most cases.
3. Earlier and adapted versions of the stage-wise development of mapping sentences have appeared in other publications.
4. There are obviously many stages and much hard work involved in developing a sampling frame, recruiting participants, and other undertakings related to identifying and accessing a study sample. I will however not go into details in this stage-wise description of the declarative mapping sentence method as I will concentrate on aspects specific to the method.
5. The importance of the selection and positioning of words in a mapping sentence cannot be overemphasised, and this includes the facets, facet elements and the connective words and phrases. This importance is due to the fact that

"words are assigned their meanings by users on the basis of their immediate collocations and semantic associations and on the basis of their cohesive collections" (Hoey, 2017, p. 148). Some quantitative researchers have ignored this warning and have developed mapping sentences without connective ontology which has resulted in a *shopping list* of variables with little holistic or everyday meaning.

6. It is now more than seven decades since Louis Guttman originated the facet theory approach to social and behavioural research (Guttman, 1944). In the seventy-five years that have come after Guttman's seminal paper a great many other publications have followed both by him and countless academics. Qualitative facet theory grew out of the research of the first author (Hackett, 2014b) and other scholars (Canter, 2019). The declarative method has been developed to be used with qualitative data. However, a slightly modified form of mapping sentence, one which incorporates a numerical outcome measure, exists and may be used with quantitative data (Canter, 1985; Guttman and Greenbaum, 1998; Levy, 1976; Lustig and Hackett, 2020a). However, the content facets for both forms of mapping sentence, if held constant, may enable the bringing together of quantitative and qualitative research (mixed-method research) within the same research project and for the findings from both methods to be directly comparable (Hackett, 2021).

7. See Cornea (2007) for an in depth consideration of the history and culture surrounding science fiction films.

References

Boyatzis, R.E. (1998) *Transforming Qualitative Information: Thematic Analysis and Code Development*, Thousand Oaks, CA: Sage Publications Inc.

Brinkmann, S. (2018) *Philosophies of Qualitative Research: Understanding Qualitative Research*, Oxford: Oxford University Press.

Canter, D. (ed.) (1985) *Facet Theory: Approaches to Social Research*, New York: Springer Verlag.

Canter, D. (2019) Qualitative Structural Theory: A Basis for Decision-Making, *International Studies of Management & Organization*, 49(3), 265–282, https://doi.org/10.1080/00208825.2019.1627705

Clarke, V., and Braun, V. (2014) Thematic Analysis, in Teo, T. (ed.) *Encyclopedia of Critical Psychology*, New York: Springer, 1947–1952.

Clarke, V., Braun, V., and Hayfield, N. (2015) Thematic Analysis, in Smith, J. (ed.) *Qualitative Psychology: A Practical Guide in Research Methods*, Thousand Oaks, CA: Sage, 222–248.

Cornea, C. (2007) *Science Fiction: Between Fantasy and Reality*, Edinburgh: Edinburgh University Press.

Cowle, K. (2018) *The Relationship Between Abstraction and Illusion: A Study of Photography and Visual Experience*, Unpublished MRes Dissertation, Birmingham City University, Birmingham, UK.

Crystal, D. (2017) The Lure of Words, in Taylor, J.R. (ed.) *The Oxford Handbook of the Word*, Oxford: Oxford University Press, 23–28.

Devine-Wright, H. (2020) Pattern-IT: A Method for Mapping Stakeholder Engagement with Complex Systems, *MethodsX*, 7, 101123, https://doi.org/10.1016/j.mex.2020.101123

Fine, M., and Torre, M.E. (2021) *Essentials of Critical Participatory Research*, Washington, DC: American Psychological Association.

Glaser, B.G. (1965) The Constant Comment Method of Qualitative Analysis, *Social Problems*, 12(4), 436–445.

Guttman, L. (1944) A Basis for Scaling Quantitative Data, *American Sociological Review*, 9(2), 139–150.

Guttman, L. (1985) Multidimensional Structuple Analysis (MSA-1) for the Classification of Cetacea: Whales, Porpoises and Dolphins, in Marcotarchino, J.F., Proth, J.M., and Janssen, J. (eds.) *Data Analysis in Real Life Environments: Ins and Outs of Solving Problems*, Amsterdam: Elsevier Science Publishers.

Guttman, R., and Greenbaum, C.W. (1998) Facet Theory: Its Development and Current Status, *European Psychologist*, 3(1), 13–36.

Hackett, P.M.W. (2013) *Fine Art and Perceptual Neuroscience: Field of Vision and the Painted Grid, Explorations in Cognitive Psychology Series*, London: Psychology Press.

Hackett, P.M.W. (2014a) An Integrated Facet Theory Mapping Sentence Descriptive Model of Contextual and Personal Life-Elements Associated with Students' Experiences of Studying Abroad, *Journal of International Students*, 4(2), 163–176.

Hackett, P.M.W. (2014b) *Facet Theory and the Mapping Sentence: Evolving Philosophy, Use and Application*, Basingstoke: Palgrave McMillan Publishers.

Hackett, P.M.W. (2016a) *Psychology and Philosophy of Abstract Art: Neuro-aesthetics, Perception and Comprehension*, Basingstoke: Palgrave McMillan Publishers.

Hackett, P.M.W. (2016b) Facet Theory and the Mapping Sentence as Hermeneutically Consistent Structured Meta-Ontology and Structured Meta-Mereology, *Frontiers in Psychology, Section Theoretical and Philosophical Psychology*, 7, 471, https://doi.org/10.3389/fpsyg.2016.00471

Hackett, P.M.W. (2017a) *The Perceptual Structure of Three-Dimensional Art, Springer Briefs in Philosophy*, New York: Springer.

Hackett, P.M.W. (2017b) Opinion: A Mapping Sentence for Understanding the Genre of Abstract Art Using Philosophical/Qualitative Facet Theory, *Frontiers in Psychology, Section Theoretical and Philosophical Psychology*, 8, October, https://doi.org/10.3389/fpsyg.2017.01731

Hackett, P.M.W. (2018) Declarative Mapping Sentence Mereologies: Categories from Aristotle to Lowe, in Hackett, P.M.W. (ed.) *Mereologies, Ontologies and Facets: The Categorial Structure of Reality*, Lanham, MD: Lexington Publishers, 135–160.

Hackett, P.M.W. (2019a) Facet Mapping Therapy: The Potential of a Facet Theoretical Philosophy and Declarative Mapping Sentences within a Therapeutic Setting, *Frontiers in Psychology, Section Psychology for Clinical Settings*, https://doi.org/10.3389/fpsyg.2019.01223

Hackett, P.M.W. (2019b) Declarative Mapping Sentences as a Co-Ordinating Framework for Qualitative Health and Wellbeing Research, *Journal of Social Science & Allied Health Professions*, 2(1), E1–E6.

Hackett, P.M.W. (2019c) *The Complexity of Bird Behaviour: A Facet Theory Approach*, Cham, CH: Springer.

Hackett, P.M.W. (2020a) *Declarative Mapping Sentences in Qualitative Research: Theoretical, Linguistic and Applied Usages*, London: Routledge.

Hackett, P.M.W. (2020b) The Declarative Mapping Sentence as a Framework for Conducting Ethnographic Health Research, in Hackett, P.M.W., and Hayre, C. (eds.) *Handbook of Ethnography in Healthcare Research*, Routledge, In Press.

Hackett, P.M.W. (2021) *Facet Theory and the Mapping Sentence: Evolving Philosophy, Use and Declarative Applications* (second and revised edition), Basingstoke: Palgrave Publishers.

Hackett, P.M.W., and Fisher, Y. (eds.) (2019) *Advances in Facet Theory Research: Developments in Theory and Application and Competing Approaches*, Lausanne, Switzerland: Frontiers Media SA.

Hackett, P.M.W., and Hayre, C. (2020) *Handbook of Ethnography in Healthcare Research*, London: Routledge.

Hackett, P.M.W., and Schwarzenbach, J.B. (2020) Black Lives Matter: Birdwatching in Central Park and the Murder of George Floyd, in Hackett, P.M.W., and Hayre, C. (eds.) *Handbook of Ethnography in Healthcare Research*, Routledge, In Press.

Hammersley, M. (2004) Analytic Induction, in Lewis-Beck, M., et al. (eds.) *The Sage Encyclopaedia of Social Science Research Methods*, Thousand Oaks, CA: Sage Publishers.

Hammersley, M., and Cooper, B. (2012) Analytic Induction Versus Qualitative Comparative Analysis, in Cooper, B., et al. (eds.) *Challenging the Qualitative-Quantitative Divide: Explorations in Case-focused Causal Analysis*, London: Continuum/Bloomsbury.

Hoey, M. (2017) Words and Their Neighbours, in Taylor, J.R. (ed.) *The Oxford Handbook of the Word*, Oxford: Oxford University Press, 141–153.

Johnston, K.M. (2011) *Science Fiction Film*, Oxford: Berg Publishers.

Koval, E., and Hackett, P.M.W. (2016) Hermeneutic Consistency, Structured Ontology and Mereology as Embodied in Facet Theory and the Mapping Sentence, *Proceedings of the 15th International Facet Theory Conference*. Jerusalem: Facet Theory Association.

Levitt, H.M. (2021) *Essentials of Critical-Constructivist Grounded Theory Research*, Washington, DC: American Psychological Association.

Levitt, H.M., Motulsky, S.L., Wertz, F.J., Morrow, S.L., and Ponterotto, J.G. (2017) Recommendations for Designing and Reviewing Qualitative Research in Psychology, *Qualitative Psychology*, 4(1), 2–22, https://doi.org/10.1037/qup0000082

Levy, S. (1976) Use of the Mapping Sentence for Coordinating Theory and Research: A Cross-Cultural Example, *Quantity and Quality*, 10, 117–125.

Lou, L., and Hackett, P.M.W. (2018) Qualitative Facet Theory and the Declarative Mapping Sentence, Contemporary Data Interpretations: Empirical Contributions in the Organizational Context, *Organization 4.1: The Role of Values in Organizations of the 21st Century*.

Lustig, K., and Hackett, P.M.W. (2020a) *Mapping Sentence Handbook*, San Francisco: Blurb Publishers.

Lustig, K., and Hackett, P.M.W. (2020b) *The Philosophy of Facet Theory Pocket Guide*, San Francisco: Blurb Publishing.

Malinowski, B. (1935) The Language of Magic in Gardening, in Malinowski, B. (eds.) *Coral Gardens and Their Magic: A Study of the Methods of Tilling the Soil and of Agricultural Rites in the Trobriand Islands* (volume II. Pt4. Div5), London: Routledge.

Morshed, G. (2020) Personal communication.

Olla, A. (2021) Bezos' Blue Origin is at Odds with Everything Star Trek Represents, Opinion: Space, *The Guardian*, 13th October 2021, www.theguardian.com/commentisfree/2021/oct/13/jeff-bezos-blue-origin-star-trek-space-william-shatner accessed: 21st October 2021.

Penley, C., Lyon, E., Spigel, L., and Bergstrom, J. (eds.) (1991) *Close Encounters: Fil, Feminism, and Science Fiction*, Minneapolis, MN: University of Minnesota Press.

Pope, C., and Mays, N. (eds.) (2019) *Qualitative Research in Health Care* (fourth edition), Hoboken, NJ: Wiley-Blackwell.

Przybylska, L. (2014) *A Mapping Sentence for the Process of Sacralisation: The Case Study of Gdynia, Prace Geograficzne, zeszyt 137*, Kraków, PL: Instytut Geografii because Gospodarki Przestrzennej UJ, https://doi.org/10.4467/20833 113PG.14.012.2157

Rabenu, E., and Hackett, P.M.W. (2017) The Philosophical and Psychological Status of Facet Theory's Mapping Sentence as Illustrated in a Case Study of Workplace Discrimination, *16th International Facet Theory Conference, Netanya Academic College*, Israel, 19th–21st June 2017.

Rapport, F., and Braithwaite, J. (eds.) (2020) *Transforming Healthcare with Qualitative Research* (Routledge Studies in Research Methods for Health and Social Welfare), London: Routledge Publishers.

Reid, C., Greaves, L., and Kirby, S. (2017) *Experience, Research, Social Change*, Toronto: Toronto University Press.

Reimer-Kirkham, S., Varcoe, C., Browne, A.J., Lynham, M.J., Khan, K.B., and McDonald, H. (2009) Critical Inquiry and Knowledge Translation: Exploring Compatibilities and Tensions, *Nursing Philosophy*, 10(3), 152–166.

Rickman, G. (ed.) (2004) *Science Fiction Film Reader*, Brisbane: Limelight.

Schwarzenbach, J.B., and Hackett, P.M.W. (2015) *Transatlantic Reflections on the Practice-Based Ph.D. in Fine Art*, New York: Routledge Publishers.

Shkoler, O., Rabenu, E., Hackett, P.M.W., and Capobianco, P.A. (2020) *International Student Mobility and Access to Higher Education* (Marketing and Communication in Higher Education), Basingstoke: Palgrave McMillan Publishers.

Terry, G., and Hayfield, N. (2021) *Essentials of Thematic Analysis*, Washington, DC: American Psychological Association.

Wihlborg, J., Edgren, G., Johansson, A., and Sivberg, B. (2019) Christina Gummesson (2019) Using the Case Method to Explore Characteristics of the Clinical Reasoning Process Among Ambulance Nurse Students and Professionals, *Nurse Education in Practice*, 35, 48–54.

Zhang, M., Gable, G., and Rai, A. (2016) Toward Principles of Construct Clarity: Exploring the Usefulness of Facet Theory in Guiding Conceptualization, *Australasian Journal of Information Systems*, 20, http://doi.org/10.3127/ajis.v20i0.1123

Znaniecki, F. (1934) *The Method of Sociology*, New York: Farrar and Rinehart.

2 Star Trek

The Original Series – "The Man Trap": The Woman Who Craves Men and the Woman Who Eats Men

Introduction

So far in this book, we have considered the background to the focus of our research, female characters in selected science fiction films and television shows, and the approach we will be taking to analyse these, the declarative mapping sentence. In this chapter, we present the first of our analyses which is an episode from the *Star Trek* series.

Star Trek: The Original Series is an American science fiction television series that first aired in the United States on 8 September 1966. The show was created by Gene Roddenberry and produced by Norway Productions from 1966 to 1967. It was originally released on 8 September 1966. The *Star Trek* franchise, consisting of eight TV series and thirteen films, is still being shown on screen. "The Man Trap" is the first episode of Season 1 in *Star Trek: The Original Series*. The story was directed by Marc Daniels and written by George Clayton Johnson.

In this episode, the crew of U.S.S. Enterprise visited planet M-113 to conduct medical examinations for the planet's only inhabitants, Professor Robert Crater (acted by Alfred Ryder) and his wife Nancy Crater (Jeanne Bal). Captain James T. Kirk (William Shatner), Chief Medical Officer Dr. Leonard McCoy (DeForest Kelley) and Darnell (Michael Zaslow) arrived at the Crater couples' research station, but when meeting Nancy, each of the Starship crew saw her as a different person. McCoy had previously been in love with Nancy, and he saw her as the young Nancy. Kirk saw her as an older version of Nancy. Darnell saw her as a completely different lady who is not Nancy at all, but a very young and attractive blonde whom he met on another planet. Later Darnell is found dead with red puncture marks on his face. Nancy was found next Darnell's body and started to cry and said that Darnell could not help eating a plant which was toxic. Spock (Leonard Nimoy) received their request to return to the Enterprise and later he performs analyses of the plant. He confirmed that the plant was poisonous

DOI: 10.4324/9781003138419-2

but that the mottled marks on Darnell's body did not come from the poison. Later on in the show, Nancy is revealed as the killer whose purpose was extracting (sucking) salt from men which resulted in their death. Crater eventually confessed that the real Nancy was actually killed by a creature who has assumed the appearance of Nancy. However, the creature liked Crater and offered love to him by transforming its body to appear to Crater as Nancy. The creature then repeatedly murdered other people by shifting its shape to appear as a variety of crew members of the ship. Later, the creature resumed Nancy's form and exploited McCoy's affection towards Nancy, flirted with him and asked him to help her. McCoy was captivated by the creature in this guise and was unable to use force against the creature or to stop the creature from attacking Kirk. At this point, Spock asked McCoy to kill the creature: "It's killing the Captain! Shoot, quick!" However, McCoy refused to shoot Nancy, so Spock hit the creature to demonstrate to McCoy that the creature he was looking at was not Nancy at all. As the creature revealed its real form, McCoy finally shot the creature and saved Kirk's life.

In addition to Nancy Crater, the other main female role in this first episode of *Star Trek* is Nyota Uhura (Nichelle Nichols). Nancy is an African American female character whose appearance in the original *Star Trek* programme is a milestone that influenced how gender and racial diversity were portrayed in subsequent filmic and televisual media. According to Eliana Dockterman, "Martin Luther King Jr. once told Nichelle Nichols, who played communications officer Uhura and who was the one to lock lips with William Shatner's Kirk for that groundbreaking kiss, that she was an inspiration to him" Dockterman (2017, p. 60). Recruiting an African American woman for the show was very bold and it advanced the depiction of gender and cultural diversity on the TV screen. Nevertheless, Uhura has little impact in eliminating gender stereotypes, since she is not one of the main protagonists and does not play an essential part in the narrative.

Using Mapping Sentence to Analyse Female Characters

Facet Profiles of Female Characters

Having presented a very terse synopsis of the episode, we will now delve more deeply into the two female characters in this episode. We start by summarising these characters and associating each character with one of the elements in each of the five facets in our final mapping sentence (see the declarative mapping sentence in Figure 1.8). It should, however, be noted that the analysis presented is the opinion of the authors, and other researchers may have opinions that vary from these. The analyses that we present are meant to be starting points in a debate that may be conducted around the profiles we propose, our justifications for these and modifications of our coding.

The facet profile we developed for Nancy Crater is given in Table 2.1.

The facet profile for Nyota Uhura is both similar to and different from that of Nancy Crater.

In Tables 2.1 and 2.2, we presented the profiles of the primary two female characters, as they are characterised by the element of the declarative mapping sentence for this study.

Table 2.1 Facet Profile for Nancy Crater

Facet profile		Details
A1	• Role: • lead role	• Nancy is the lead role. • The entire episode is about her killing men. • She occupies the most important role.
B3	• Sexual Appearance: • overly emphasised	• Her sexual appearance is overtly emphasised. • Her appearance is contrived to satisfy men's desire.
C3	• Bad Woman: • femme fatale	• She is a bad woman and a femme fatale character in the plot.
D3	• Physical Strength: • weak	• She is physically weak. • Although she killed men, she did not use her own physical strength to do this. • She used her beauty to lure men.
E3	• Personal Authority: • fully dependent	• She is fully dependent on men for salt intimating that she depended on men to live.

Table 2.2 Facet Profile for Nyota Uhura

Facet profile		Details
A2	Role: support role	Uhura does not play the most important part in the episode but plays a supporting role.
B3	Sexual Appearance: overly emphasised	We are driven to look at her appearance and beauty over her other attributes.
C1	Bad Woman: not bad	She is not a bad woman.
D3	Physical Strength: Weak	In terms of her physical strength, she is very weak. She stayed on-board the Enterprise all the time. She was not included in the adventure/action scenes.
E3	Personal Authority: fully dependent	She does not make decisions but simply passes on information to help the male characters make decisions.

Profile Summary

In Table 2.3, we present together the facet element profiles for the two female characters we evaluated. These two profiles were as follows.

In Table 2.3, it can be seen that the two characters were given the same ratings on facets B, D and E. In these cases, both Uhura and Crater were seen as: facet B (physical appearance) where both women's sexuality and appearance were overly emphasised; facet D (physical strength) where both characters were rated as weak; facet E (personal authority) where both women were seen as possessing little or no autonomy. Thus, both the main female characters, one of which was on the side of right and the other one was the show's "baddie," had their physical appearance, their physical weakness and their lack of personal authority emphasised. However, on the other two facets, the two women received different ratings. The first facet (facet A) was an assessment of the degree to which the characters played lead roles. Nancy Crater was seen to take a lead role while Nyota Uhura played a supporting part. In this show, the alien aggressor was played by a woman and her role was central to the plot, while the other main female character was on the side of good but her role was only minor. The two women also achieved different profile scores for facet C which was an assessment of the degree to which the roles portrayed the women as bad women. Nancy Crater was indeed seen to be a bad woman, while Uhura was not and it is interesting to note that only lead woman was cast in the role of an alien aggressor.

However, the assigning of profile elements to a character is only the start of using a declarative mapping sentence to analyse movie characters. The next stage of this process is to unpack the meaning of and the reasons for the allocation of a character to an element in a facet profile. In the following section, we will do this by considering Nancy Crater and Nyota Uhura in terms of the facet elements for the declarative mapping sentence.

Facet A: Female Role

Nancy Crater (A1 – Lead Role)

Nancy is the female lead and therefore was allotted to the A1 element. She is central to the story. The whole episode is about her using her sexuality to

Table 2.3 Comparison of Profiles for Two Female Characters

Character	Facet A	Facet B	Facet C	Facet D	Facet E
Nancy Crater	A1	B3	C3	D3	E3
Nyota Uhura	A2	B3	C1	D3	E3

lure and trap men. Nancy is a monster who can transform her body to each man's ideal type of woman. Different men see Nancy as different images. McCoy fantasised about Nancy earlier in his life, so in his eyes, Nancy was exactly the same as the young Nancy he knew before. In Kirk's eyes, Nancy was an older woman. However, Darnell saw Nancy as a different person, a very attractive young girl whom he met on another planet. Nancy is all men's fantasy, and she is accomplished in using her looks to lure men. Darnell followed Nancy outside but was killed by Nancy. Nancy needed to extract salt from men's body in order to live. The entire episode is about her killing men. She is playing the most important role.

Nyota Uhura (A2 – Support Role)

In terms of the role facet (A), we believe Nyota Uhura to be typified as an A2 (a female support role). This is because she was excluded from doing significant activities during the episode. There are so many limitations to her role, such as not leaving the ship or participating more fully in parts of the programme that drove the narrative, not being allowed to make decisions or to undertake essential work. In addition, she does not play an important role in comparison to her male counterparts. Instead, she is only a support female character who assisted male characters in their important jobs, and she essentially played the role of a telephone operator from the era in which the episode was made (this was a predominantly female job). Her role of assisting men to do their job was demonstrated in scenes in which she answered calls from Kirk and McCoy when they needed help from the ship, but then she transferred the calls to Spock to handle and to solve the problem. Although Uhura was the Communications Officer, she had neither the power to make decisions for the ship nor the capability to help Kirk and McCoy. In the end, Spock made the decisions and offered rational help to Kirk and McCoy.

As Amanda Keeler (2019) points out

> it must be acknowledged that *TOS* (*Star Trek: The Original Series*) presented its own idealized world that made women and actors of colour into central characters, yet overlooked the need to tell the stories of how these characters achieved their positions.
>
> (Keeler, 2019, p. 148)

It is clear to see that the filmmakers made Uhura a moderately important role but did not give her a chance to tell her own story or to show her own characteristics. Moreover, Uhura was called a Communications Officer onboard but only did unimportant and simple jobs which reflected the roles of women in the workforce at that time. Uhura stayed on-board the Starship most of the time and answered radio calls but did not engage in making decisions. We should appreciate and acknowledge that Uhura being an African American female truly helps to construct a bridge enhancing race and gender diversity in television and film works. However, although her appearance is commendable, at least in the first episode, her existence does not help break the traditional gender- and race-based stereotypes but rather, in a way, reinforces the subservient roles of women and people of colour.

It seems likely that creators of the show wanted to use actress Nichelle Nichols' African American female status as an advertisement of the progressive nature of their show and to highlight gender and racial diversity even though Lieutenant Uhura's influence is still somewhat restricted. Thus, it is probably only the presence of actor Nichelle Nichols in the show that offers gender diversity and exposure, since her character and the role she plays are neither substantive nor progressive. Also, being a secondary role means that she had a diminished impact on the viewers.

Facet B: Sexual Appearance

Nancy Crater (B3 – Overly Emphasised)

Nancy Crater is also the alien monster, and we allocated her to element 3 for the B Facet, as her sexuality was overly emphasised. This is a major component of her role, as she appeared to any man who looked at her as a reflection of that man's fantasies and as the most alluring vision of a woman for that particular man. The *Star Trek* episode "The Man Trap" therefore does not help break gender stereotypes, because the episode signifies that women gain their power by adopting an appearance that satisfies men's desires. In "The Man Trap," Nancy changed herself into different female bodies and adopted different faces in order to cater to men's imaginations, implying that women should take any form that men want them to be. In this sense, the episode indicates that men decide what women should be or look like, and thus, women should pander to men's sexual desire in order to achieve their desired aims. Women should not be themselves but be what men want them to be. Nancy is the dream woman of all men, since she can be anything that any man required her to be. Nancy is a warm lover to be loved, a cool lady to be respected and a beautiful young girl to have fun with, but she is also a monster who uses her beauty to get what she wants. Thus, we categorise her as B3, since her body is not her own but what men think or want her to be, and her appearance is very much emphasised on the screen.

Nyota Uhura (B3 – Overly Emphasised)

We rated Uhura's sexual appearance as being overly emphasised (B3), the same profile assignment as we gave to Nancy Crater. The reason we allotted her to this element is because her costume emphasises her feminine traits and reinforces her difference from her male colleagues. This may be seen as being degrading and also to deepen gender stereotypes. In one scene, her female subservience was stressed when Uhura walked up to Spock and adopted a lower physical position. She looked up to Spock with a pair of admiring eyes. Uhura then started to talk about emotions and waited for Spock to tell her that she is attractive. What is perhaps most important is that this is the scene in which she first appeared in the episode and which established her position in relation to male crew members from the start.

Uhura wore *cats' eye* makeup, a pair of showy golden earrings, and a red mini skirt and a tight-fitting top. As Andres (2013) says, "the nature of their uniforms makes it just as obvious that they are women." Although the show wants to express gender equality, Andres believes that "the clothes and styles of the characters expresses the contrary" (Andres, 2013, p. 642). The costumes of female characters which demonstrate obvious femininity are a complete contrast to the men in Star Trek who are dressed in comfortable, practical and somewhat casual clothes. According to Andres, "The women's dresses are 'less' functional uniforms than the shirt and pants of the men, which implies that women are 'less' functional as well" (Andres, 2013, p. 642). The mini skirt marks Uhura's female attributes which perpetuate gender roles. Hence, by looking at Uhura's costume, it is obvious to see that her sexuality is overtly emphasised, because viewers are driven to her appearance and beauty over everything else. Therefore, we categorise Uhura as B3, as her sexuality is extremely obvious and overtly emphasised.

Facet C: Bad Woman

Nancy Crater (C3 – Femme Fatale)

The femme fatale or bad woman who leads men astray is our third facet. Nancy is clearly a femme fatale character, and for facet C, we assigned her to this element (C3). Nancy, the salt sucking monster, is a typically dangerous female character who traps men by assuming their desired female images. However, this immoral story of a female monster getting salt by sucking the life out of men expresses a misogynous concept. Franich (2016) notes in the first *Star Trek* episode that bad guys don't really exist, as the creature is just doing what it has to do, seeking salt in order to stay alive, and while it might be intelligent but it also has to fulfil its basic animal needs and do what it has to do to survive. Nevertheless, we find it hard to agree that there are no bad guys. It seems that sucking the salt out of someone, even if the creature doing this is biologically impelled rather than making a cognitive or an emotionally based choice, can be defined as a highly negative action if not bad. When Nancy turns from a desired woman into an animal, she occupies a different position in an animal world as a non-human predator. Does such a transition reflect upon how women are seen to have animal power over men by appealing to their desires? We believe that the way the woman turns into a creature that consumes men is rooted in misogynistic culture and conceptions.

Nyota Uhura (C1 – Not Bad)

In reference to facet 3, we assigned Uhura to the facet element of not being a bad woman (C1). Comparing Uhura with the female monster who kills men for the energy, Uhura is much nicer to the men, and audiences would probably not think of her as a bad woman. While Uhura is not bad in the episode, she does not have enough meaningful dialogue or parts in stories to show her personality. Hence, we only know her as a woman who is not bad. Thus, even though we rate Uhura as C1, there is a need to provide more storylines that show her personality and her character and abilities.

Facet D: Physical Strength

Nancy Crater (D3 – Weak)

In terms of the facet of physical strength, we allotted Nancy Crater to the D3 element of the facet, which indicated that she is physically weak and that she cannot protect herself. When Nancy appeared as a woman, she was alluring and vulnerable and needed protection. It is only when she transformed into the man-killing alien that she gained any physical strength, and this strength was derived from the ability to blind men to her true nature: she gained strength from the men she killed as a monster and as a woman she was weak.

Nyota Uhura (D3 – Weak)

We mark Uhura as D3 due to her physical weakness in "The Man Trap." She stayed on-board the Starship Enterprise all the time during the episode doing unimportant jobs and being excluded from the outside dangerous tasks and the episode's action scenes. Her menial jobs and dialogues did not reflect the increasing job opportunities and the improved female roles in the 1960s, but her role appeared to be more consistent with women's employment situation in the 1950s. During the time when women's roles were very much over-looked, *Star Trek: The Original Series* placed Uhura on-board aside with male counterparts. However, as Campagna (2018) claims, gender takes on an anti-quated conceptualisation in *Star Trek*, one which didn't reflect the changes in society in regards to gender. "*Star Trek* holds on to a very strict set of gender norms that would be much more appropriate to liken to the 1950s rather than the 1960s" (Campagne, 2018, p. 10). In the 1950s, women were expected to stay in the home doing domestic work or to have jobs in low salaries, such as secretaries and store workers. "As opposed to the 1950s, the 1960s was a time during which there was a growing 2nd wave of feminism" (Campagna, 2018, p. 11). Along with the second wave of feminism, women were granted more possibilities, including occupation opportunities that "were not avail-able previously to them" (Campagna, 2018, p. 13). Thus, if the makers of the *Original Star Trek* series wanted to empower women in society, they could have taken this opportunity to give Uhura some crucial and meaningful work.

Uhura is submissive and subordinate to the male characters playing "pas-sive roles both in and out of dangerous situations," while the men "are meant for leadership roles" (Campagna, 2018, p. 10). The men in the show are the ones to take action. All crew members who landed and went to on-the-spot investigation were men, whereas women were kicked out from adventur-ous situations. While Kirk, McCoy and Darnell went to the new planet for adventure, Uhura was left on-board; this is also related to Uhura's physical weakness and inconvenience of being outside in a short skirt.

Facet E: Personal Authority

Nancy Crater (E3 – Fully Dependent)

"The Man Trap" shows that the female character Nancy Crater relies on men in order to stay alive. Such a storyline intensifies gender stereotypes and a female dependency narrative. In fact, Nancy is fully dependent upon men in all ways which means we allocated her to the E3 facet element in her profile. An illustration of her dependency is shown when James T. Kirk found out that Nancy was the murderer of his crew members. At this point, Nancy asks McCoy for help demonstrating her use of men to protect her. Additionally, Nancy relied on men for almost everything, especially the salt that she needed to stay alive and metaphorically for her continued existence and protection.

Nyota Uhura (E3 – Fully Dependent)

We categorise Uhura also as E3 (a fully dependent female character) on the facet of personal authority. We did this because when compared to her male counterparts who had challenging, exciting and active jobs, Uhura was assigned with trivial jobs, and she was fully dependent on men for making decision to which she responded. Lieutenant Uhura worked as a Communications Officer. Although her job title sounded somewhat significant, the work she did was not vital to the storyline. When Kirk, McCoy, Spock, etc., needed help when they are engaging in some heroic deed, Uhura was supposed to be the one to communicate with them. Nonetheless, Spock was actually the one directly talking to them. Probably we should just call Uhura as a receptionist who did not really answer the phone calls. Thus, Uhura being as a female lieutenant who plays very little role in the show's storyline was also an outsider in the male-dominated world. The question may even be asked of what was the point for her being called as a communications officer, and what exactly was her exact role?

Conclusion

In conclusion, the casting of an African American woman, Uhura, in the initial episode of *Star Trek* helped to build a bridge to greater gender equality in future television programmes and films. However, the bridge is quite limited, since Uhura does not play an important part in moving the story along. Additionally, Uhura's passive job, illogical dialogue and overtly cliched feminine and hackneyed sexual mini dress are all elements that perpetuate traditional gender roles. It may have been too much to ask of a commercial television programme at the time *Star Trek* first appeared to have given a woman of colour a more important job to do in the series. As for Nancy, the femme fatale monster, who changes herself into different men's desires and negates her own identity, she reinforces the dominant patriarchal ideology of women both appealing to the weakness of men and needing men to survive. At the same time, Nancy murdered men to achieve her own purpose, which presents a misogynous ideology to viewers. The other women in the show play a largely nonspeaking and insignificant role while usually being clad in sexually provocative clothes. Much can be done to improve gender representations in *Star Trek: The Original Series* and to avoid gender stereotypes. We have to acknowledge that Uhura clearly brought a black female actor and character to the attention of the mass audience at a time when white men were still the mainstream. Her role was perhaps the start of a future vision of gender and racial equality during a time where gender and racial inequality were dominant.

The episode also portrays many differences between the behaviours of women and men. For instance, the only thing Uhura was doing while everyone else was working on-board was having a conversation with Spock asking for his opinion about her attractiveness. Uhura and Spock's interactions reflect the differences in the representation of women and men. Uhura represents emotional, sympathetic and subordinate women. Spock embodies men's characteristics of logical, reasonable, strong and calm behaviour. Uhura walked to stand next to Spock and looked up to him: "Mister Spock, sometimes I think if I hear that word frequency once more, I'll cry." To which Spock replied, "Cry?" and looks bemused as Spock is logical and never cries. Uhura's language is shown as illogical. The screenwriting here emphasises stereotypical gender attribute that women cry a lot and are irrational. In addition, when both Uhura and Spock heard that a crewman had died, they had totally different reactions. Uhura was shocked and stopped for a moment, but Spock showed no expression on his face. Uhura was even more shocked to Spock's calm reaction, and she said, "That means that somebody is dead, and you just sit there." Spock responded, "Lieutenant, my demonstration of concern will not change what happened. The transporter room is very well-manned, and they will call if they need my assistance." Uhura became even more emotional in reaction to Spock's cold-blooded response. In these and other scenes, the episode stresses the cognitive and emotional difference between men and women, and reinforces mid-twentieth century's gender stereotypes.

Social standards have experienced big changes over the past 50 years, and simultaneously, televisions and movies have placed increasing attention on advocating gender and racial equality. During more than 50 years since the 1966 debut of the original *Star Trek* series to contemporary media works, audiences have developed a new standard through which they view social norms and gender representations in TV shows and movies. In reference to this first episode of *Star Trek*, we believe that the show should not be judged too harshly and that the inadequacies are a product of the era in which the programme was made and demonstrates the differences between the past and the present. This episode allows us to appreciate how far we have come in the 50 years that have passed since the programme's making. It also shows how we have gained a greater awareness regarding gender representations in films, televisions and even our daily lives. However, we should not simply be accepting of gender roles, because they are from the past. Rather, we should use such programmes to remind us of these differences and to stress the importance of avoiding these gender inequalities in movie making. By recruiting and including a woman of colour in the very first episode, "The Man Trap," *Star Trek: The Original Series*, certainly made progress in enhancing the intersectionality of gender and racial diversity, but it fails to really make a difference in changing patriarchal ideologies. Thus, *Star Trek: The Original Series* has a long way to go in altering patriarchal standpoints because of its unequal and stereotypical gender representations.

References

Andres, K. (2013) Fashion's Final Frontier: The Correlation of Gender Roles and Fashion in Star Trek. *Culture Unbound*, 5, 639–649, Linkoping University Electronic Press. http://www.cultureunbound.ep.liu.se

Campagne, N. (2018) *The Final Frontier: Examining Gender and Race in the 1960s Through Star Trek*, History Undergraduate Publications and Presentations, 10–13. https://pilotscholars.up.edu/hst_studpubs/20

Dockterman, E. (2017) In a Quantum Leap, Star Trek Becomes a Female Enterprise, *Time Off*, 59–60.

Franich, D. (2016) Star Trek Turns 50: A Look Back at the Desperately Sad First Episode, *EW.com*, 8th September 2016, https://ew.com/article/2016/09/08/star-trek-50th-anniversary-first-episode-man-trap/

Keeler, A. (2019) Visible/invisible: Female Astronauts and Technology in Star Trek: Discovery and National Geographic's Mars, *Science Fiction Film and Television*, 12(1), 148, Liverpool University Press.

3 Blade Runner

Do Sexualised Androids Dream of Gender Equality?

Introduction

Blade Runner was written by Hampton Fancher and David Peoples and is a loose adaptation of Philip K. Dick's classic 1968 science fiction book, *Do Androids Dream of Electric Sheep?* The movie is a neo-noir science fiction film set in a dystopian future in Los Angeles in 2019. It is worth noting that this dystopia is emphasised by the fact that, in the movie, the powerful rich has already left the Earth and has emigrated to the Off-world. In *Studying Blade Runner*, Redmond (2008) describes the *Blade Runner* world as a nightmare:

> Los Angeles 2019 is largely an urban nightmare – a nightmare fleshed out of the materials of globalisation, capitalism, cyberpunk, and noir, so that its neon and concrete veins and arteries appear clogged up and yet leaky, pouring despair onto its inhabitants.
>
> (Redmond, 2008, p. 49)

Stepping into this *Blade Runner* interspace, the foggy city landscape is filled with humid rain, which blurs and distorts our vision. Looking up in the sky above, this decaying urban space can be seen as the fast-flying vehicles travelling between esoterically shaped polygonal skyscrapers. Neon lights, sharp shadows, cyber machines and punk costumes all suggest a futuristic cyberpunk environment cast within a decaying urban atmosphere.

There are three important female characters in the movie. The first two of these are Pris (played by Daryl Hannah) and Zhora (Joanna Cassidy). Both of these characters are human-made cyborgs, also known in the movie as replicants. In this film, Rick Deckard (Harrison Ford) is a police detective who is asked to hunt four replicants who are attempting to escape, including two female robots, Pris and Zhora, and two male cyborgs, Roy Batty (Rutger Hauer) and Leon Kowalski (Brion James). Pris and Zhora are presented

DOI: 10.4324/9781003138419-3

as both strong and sexual women who use their sexuality to captivate men. The mission of Pris is to use her sexual attractions to make J. F. Sebastian assist them in getting to Dr. Eldon Tyrell (Joe Turkel). They are travelling to see Dr. Tyrell, as he is the founder and corporate head of the Tyrell Corporation, also known as the engineer of all replicants, humanoid slaves.

In our analysis, we consider the roles played by the replicants Pris and Zhora, how these female characters' sexuality are expressed in the film and why the filmmakers decided to punish the characters by handing them a death sentence. There is a third major female character in the movie, Rachael, played by Sean Young, and she is also part of our analysis. Rachel is different from the two femme fatale character cyborgs. Rachel is a vulnerable and kind android who falls in love with Rick. She is beautiful, and she also uses her softness and feminine attributes to lure Rick and can therefore be seen as being very different from but also similar to both Pris and Zhora. An interesting question is therefore, why would the filmmaker decide that Rachael is a good cyborg while the other two replicants are considered to be bad? The answer is perhaps that the patriarchal nature of the film locates a woman's position as being noble rather than evil dependent upon their evidencing weakness in the way that the character of Rachel does. Furthermore, to a great extent, Rick appeals to Rachael because of her vulnerability. It is powerless she possesses of being powerless that makes Rick wants to protect and save her. We will talk more about these issues later in this chapter

Using Mapping Sentence to Analyse Female Characters

In the previous section, we have very briefly introduced the film *Blade Runner* and its three major female characters. In the following sections, we will commence our analyses of the three women using declarative mapping sentence and producing the profiles the mapping sentences yield for each character.

Facet Profiles of Female Characters

The first character we consider is that of the cyborg Pris, and in Table 3.1, we display how we considered that Pris was characterised by the elements of each of the mapping sentence's five facets.

We then performed a similar series of analyses for the character of Zhora and our results are shown in Table 3.2.

The last of the female character profiles we developed was for Rachel and this is presented in Table 3.3.

Table 3.1 Facet Profile for Pris

Facet profile	Details
A2 • Role: • support role	• Pris plays a support role. • She is an important character, but not as important as Roy, a male replicant. • She listens to Roy, the male replicant leader. • She supports Roy's plan. • The storyline could continue without her.
B3 • Sexual Appearance: • overly emphasised	• Her sexual appearance is overtly emphasised. • She is designed as a "sex machine." • Her costume strongly emphasises her sexualised body. • Her dressing style is meant to appeal to male viewers.
C3 • Bad Woman: • femme fatale	• She is a Femme fatale character who uses men to achieve her purpose.
D3 • Physical Strength: • weak	• Physically she is shown as weak. • Deckard still beats Pris in a fight and is physically stronger.
E3 • Personal Authority: • fully dependent	• She is fully dependent. • She listens to and obeys Roy, the male leader of the group of replicants who are trying to escape.

Table 3.2 Facet Profile for Zhora

Facet profile	Details
• A2 • Role: • support role	She listens to the male replicant leader. She supports Roy's plan. The storyline could continue without her.
• B3 • Sexual Appearance: • overly emphasised	Her sexual appearance is overtly emphasised. Her costume shows her hyper-sexuality. There are scenes where she is almost naked.
• C3 • Bad Woman: • femme fatale	She is portrayed as a bad woman and a femme fatale.
• D3 • Physical Strength: • Weak	Deckard beats and kills Zhora in a fight.
• E3 • Personal Authority: • fully dependent	Zhora is shown as not having a mind of her own. Roy leads several replicants who want to escape, including Zhora. Zhora follows what Roy wants her to do.

Table 3.3 Facet Profile for Rachael

Facet profile		Details
• A1	Role: lead role	She is the female protagonist. She is meant to be the heroine who will fall in love with the male protagonist and who needs to be saved by her male lover.
• B2	Sexual Appearance: moderately emphasised	Her sexual appearance is moderately emphasised. Her makeup and dressing style play an important part and draw viewers' attention to her being a beautiful woman.
• C1	Bad Woman: not bad	She is not a bad woman.
• D3	Physical Strength: Weak	She is physically weak and needs Deckard to protect her.
• E3	Personal Authority: fully dependent	Her job as a secretary emphasises that she listens to her male leader – Dr. Eldon Tyrell. She is submissive to Deckard which is what makes her a "good woman"; When Rachael knows that she is also a replicant, she decides to escape, but she is not so strong enough to make the decision herself and seeks Deckard's help.

Having set out the profiles of our three characters, we did not discuss how each facet enables us to describe these women and the roles they play. We commence with Facet A: Role.

Facet A: Role

The first character we analyse is Pris and this will be followed by Zhora and then Rachel: we follow this ordering throughout this chapter.

Pris (A2 – Support Role)

The character of Pris performs in a supporting role (A2) in *Blade Runner*. She is an important character in the film. However, when compared to other roles, such as that of her male colleague, Roy, Pris is not as essential to the film's overall plot. Pris listens to Roy, the male replicant leader, and she supports his plans and carries out his orders. If Pris was removed from the film, the storyline could still go ahead without her unlike the character of the male leader, Roy.

Zhora (A2 – Support Role)

Zhora's part is a female supporting role, so we rate her as A2. In a similar way to Pris, Zhora's actions are driven by the male replicant leader Roy's decision. Zhora only exists as a sidekick who plays a supporting role that is an even less significant role than Pris. Zhora does not make important decisions or contribute ideas, and as with the character of Pris, Zhora also supports Roy's plan in order to help herself find a way to escape. The storyline can definitely progress without her.

Rachael (A1 – Lead Role)

Rachael is the female protagonist, and in our ratings, she is A1. She is also the romantic heroine who will fall in love with, and needs to be saved by, the male hero, Rick Deckard. Without her, the story of romance is not able to take place.

We now turn to the second facet of our research, facet B, which is concerned with the sexualised appearance of the female characters. We take some time on this facet, as the sexualised appearance of female characters is a central aspect of *Blade Runner*: this becomes apparent when reading our explanations for our ratings on this facet.

Facet B: Sexual Appearance

Pris (B3 – Overly Emphasised)

We allotted Pris to the profile of B3, because the sexuality of her appearance is overtly emphasised. Indeed, she has been made to be consumed as a "sex machine." Her costume is strongly accentuated in the film to show her sexiness, and her style of dressing is aimed to appeal to the male viewers.

It seems reasonable to state that Blade Runner degrades women by objectifying the female characters in the movie. Pris made her debut in the film as an image on a computer screen, which introduces to the audience the fact that she is a robotic product rather than being human. Officer Bryant pointed at her picture and called her a "basic pleasure model," and he followed this with a pitiless description of Pris being a "standard item for military clubs in the outer colonies." From Pris' initial appearance in the film, Pris is reduced into an object by the male officer, Bryant. In commenting about this, Des Roches (2017) writes, "Referring to Pris as a 'standard item' is, in itself, blatantly objectifying" (Des Roches, 2017, p. 15). When she is defined as no more than an object, she lost her female sexuality (which means that she is something less than a woman), her physical cyborg body and even her status of being a living being. And more specifically, she has been made no more than an item for men's sexual needs. The movie can therefore be seen to be with little female roles by depicting Pris as a sexual object for male desire.

Moreover, the film made female roles into sexualised images to satisfy men's desire to look longingly at women. As Mulvey (1975) demonstrates, in the patriarchal culture, man who is the active bearer of the gaze enjoys the visual pleasure of female projection with the woman becoming the object of the gaze. Far from breaking this patriarchal visual pleasure expectation, *Blade Runner* displays female androids as sexual objects and thus favours the male gaze. In other words, Blade Runner follows the patriarchal standpoint to focus on showing female's sexuality, and thus suggests that women should be looked at with sexual desire by men. Audiences do not view Pris as a whole, because she is overtly sexualised and divided into sexual body parts. For instance, the film continues to overlook Pris' status of being a woman by directing audiences to focus on Pris' hypersexuality and we therefore rate Pris as B3. At this point, Pris is not seen as a complete woman with the male gaze resting upon her emphasised and sexualised and displayed body parts. Ridley Scott also mentioned in an interview about *Blade Runner* that "if this patriarchal technology could create artificial women, then they'd surely design them to be young and sexually attractive" (Laura Mulvey, 1975). This acknowledges that his film was based on patriarchal ideology, and at the same time, that Scott created the female robots to be sexually attractive for the mass male audience. Thus, the movie presents Pris' sexuality for the male gaze, which strengthens the unspoken gender rules in patriarchal society.

Zhora (B3 – Overly Emphasised)

We also decided that Zhora was B3 on the second facet of our analysis. This was because, as in the case of Pris, her sexual appearance was overtly emphasised, and her costume is meant to show her hyper-sexuality. There are scenes where Zhora wears a transparent jacket which fails to cover her naked body.

In addition, the film not only highlights female sexuality for the male gaze but also overlooks women by marginalising them. The female replicants are excluded from the normal society and are regarded as society's lower classes, a point emphasised by Rebekah Brammer who notes that the female replicant "is frequently situated in underworld settings such as bars or nightclubs, places on the edge of or outside 'normal' society" (Brammer, 2016, p. 100).

Zhora works as an exotic dancer in a seedy nightclub, work which revolves explicitly around the male gaze. She drapes a snake around her neck and has facial diamond-like stickers all over her face and her nearly naked body, and at this moment, Zhora is not only a sexual object but her body also becomes a tool through which she makes her living. She is a lower-class woman who has to use her sexuality, dancing naked for the male's desire. Her dancing job "is yet another example of women being both objectified and hypersexualized by the men around them, and again, works towards the perpetuation of patriarchal ideologies" (Roches, 2017, p. 17). However, in contrast to Zhora, the male replicants, Roy and Leon, do not have work that they have to undertake every day, but rather they display their extreme masculinity by fighting with the cop, Deckard. Accordingly, *Blade Runner* relegates women to a lower position than men by marginalising them from the normal society and allocating them into a lower class who must undertake demeaning work to survive.

Rachael (B2 – Moderately Emphasised)

The last female character that we evaluate in terms of facet B is Rachael and we consider the emphasis placed upon her sexual appearance to be B2. This assessment is due to her sexual appearance being moderately emphasised in the movie. However, her makeup and dressing style do play an important part and draw viewers' attention to her being a beautiful woman, and the movie sets the criteria that in order to be a good woman, Rachael must be visually pleasurable.

Rachel is similar to the other two female characters in that she is made to satisfy men's visual desires. Although it may be argued that, in the film, attempts are made not to make her role as sexual as the other two main women in the film, viewers cannot help but notice the emphasis that is placed upon her beauty. Rachel's beauty and sexuality are major components of her character even though she does not necessarily have to expose her body. In the scene where Rachael first appears on the screen, the audience looks at Rachael walking towards Deckard in an all-black leather suit, appearing both slender and elegant. As she approaches closer, her finely tailored clothing becomes more apparent. The camera can be seen to "collect" her body and her makeup from a full body shot to a more focused close-up shot, which motivates the audience to study her sexualised image more closely and to notice her attractive hairstyle and her delicate makeup, which emphasises her twinkling eyes and magenta glossy lips. Although her sexuality is not as overtly emphasised as the other two characters, her makeup and dressing style play an important part and draw audiences' attention to her being a beauty. Nevertheless, while being pretty, Rachael has to follow the male's lead.

Facet C: Bad Woman

Pris (C3 – Femme Fatale)

On facet C, we rated Pris as C3, because she is clearly a femme fatale character who uses men to achieve her purpose. This claim is supported by her luring and trapping the character of J. F. Sebastian so as to achieve her own purposes. Pris pretended to fear J. F. Sebastian in order to get close to him. Pris then started her plan to lure Sebastian to help her and the character Roy to escape. Indeed, Pris does not even like J. F. Sebastian but only uses Sebastian as a tool to get near to Eldon Tyrell, the male character who is cast as the brilliant maker and engineer of all robots: who gives life to the female characters we are considering in our review. As soon as Sebastian helps them get inside of Eldon Tyrell's building, Pris abandoned Sebastian and helps Roy to kill Tyrell.

Zhora (C3 – Femme Fatale)

In our assessment, Zhora is C3, what we are calling a bad woman and a femme fatale character. Although Zhora is a sidekick and a support female character, she plays the part of being a bad woman who fights and tries to kill those on the righteous side, such as Rick Deckard. In a similar manner to Pris, Zhora uses her beauty and her sexually emphasised body to attract and to lure men in order that she can survive. Her goal is to help Roy achieve his plan.

Rachael (C1 – Not Bad)

When she is compared to Pris and Zhora, Rachael is the female lead role, and she is clearly what may be termed a "good" woman, C1. Rachael's character is one of an innocent woman, who, like Rick, is on the righteous side of the story's plot. When Leon chases Rick in order to extract revenge, Rachael helps Rick by shooting Leon. This was the first time Rachael had used a gun, which she did because of her romantic feelings towards Rick.

Facet D: Physical Strength

The fourth facet in the profiles we constructed of the female characters in Blade Runner addressed their physical strength.

Pris (D3 – Weak)

Even though in the movie attempts are made to present Pris as a super robot, we still categorise her as D3, since Pris' physical strength is not at the same level as the male characters. Even though the film states that replicants are stronger and more flexible than human beings, Deckard still defeats and finally kills Pris. Regardless of the fact that she is a robot, ultimately, she is still a woman who cannot beat a man and in front of whom she becomes powerless and weak. Blade Runner thus reinforces a patriarchal ideology by placing women in a lower position than men, demonstrating that women are powerless to men and should fear them. In the film, women's power is erased and men are positioned at the top of the power system, signalling that women should not only be sexual images, but they should also have less power than men and ultimately be subordinate to men.

The film's viewer first sees Pris' slowly moving body outside from a computer screen as she walks down a dark and confined alley; soft music is playing in the background. Pris dresses herself in a sexy punk style and audiences are encouraged to spy upon her fuzzy short hair, leopard-print coat, and black-stocking clad legs and her exposed thighs. Scared, she stubs out her cigarette and hides herself in a garbage dump waiting for J. F. Sebastian to find her although she runs away as he approaches her. When Sebastian calls after her to tell her that she forgot her bag, she walks back to Sebastian with hesitation and fear, a fear that embodies the idea that women should be powerless and physically weaker than men: "This fear in response to the male suggests that men of all kind are to be feared" (Roches, 2017, p. 16). In this sense, the film conveys an imbalanced gender power and further perpetuates the notion that women are subordinates of men.

Zhora (D3 – Weak)

On the physical strength facet, Zhora was assessed as D3, implying that she is rather weak. As we have already stated, even though the film emphasises that replicant's bodies are stronger and more flexible than human beings, Zhora's body is not physically as strong as Deckard (a human male) who angrily hunts her down and demonstrates his extreme strength. Zhora appeared weak and helpless in front of Deckard who realises that she cannot defeat which leads her to run away from instead of fighting.

Rachael (D3 – Weak)

We assessed Rachael to be D3, because she is physically weaker than male characters and submissive towards Deckard. Rachael is subservient to Deckard, which is shown as a "good trait" and which makes her into a "good woman." When Rachael learns that she is a replicant, she is frightened that she will be hunted down by the police and so she turns to Deckard for help. This is because Rachael is not strong enough to escape on her own and her physical weakness drives her to seek help from a man.

Facet E: Personal Authority

Pris (E3 – Fully Dependent)

The last of our five facets is that of personal authority, and on this, Pris was categorised as E3 because she is fully dependent on Roy. In *Blade Runner*, Pris showed neither independent thinking nor the making of crucial decisions on her own, and her personal authority is erased from the film.

Zhora (E3 – Fully Dependent)

Zhora is also categorised as E3 on facet E. She is fully dependent on Roy to make decisions and to guide her. Zhora simply follows what a man wants her to do.

Rachael (E3 – Fully Dependent)

Rachael is assessed to be E3, since, in terms of her personal authority, she is fully dependent. On the one hand, although Rachael's job as a secretary is less demeaning than Zhora's job as a nightclub dancer, Rachael follows the male leader – Dr. Eldon Tyrell. On the other hand, Rachel is a submissive lover who does what the man wants and acts in a way that satisfies men's pride in being leaders. This is shown when Deckard kissed Rachael without her consent, which, we considered, almost felt like a "rape" scene. However, differently to other female replicants, Rachael does not fight back. When Deckard pushed Rachael to the window and commanded her to say, "I want you," Rachael showed her compliance by doing what he asked. Ultimately, her vulnerability becomes the reason for her being saved rather than being killed and her submissive personality becomes what makes her into a "good woman." Consequently, what the movie tells the viewer is that a good woman should be both visually pleasurable and mentally and physically obedient to the men.

Profile Summary

We have now completed our rating of the female characters in *Blade Runner* on the five facets of our mapping sentence. In order to allow easier comparisons of the characters, in Table 3.4, we present the three characters' ratings on the five facets.

Table 3.4 Comparison of Profiles for Three Female Characters

	Facet A	*Facet B*	*Facet C*	*Facet D*	*Facet E*
Pris	A2	B3	C3	D2	E3
Zhora	A2	B3	C3	D2	E3
Rachael	A1	B2	C1	D3	E3

Legend

Facet A: Lead/Support Role
Facet B: Sexual Appearance
Facet C: Bad Woman
Facet D: Physical Strength
Facet E: Personal Authority

It can be seen in Table 3.4 that Pris and Zhora had identical profiles suggesting that the two support characters played similar roles with very similar characteristics and who behaved in a similar way. Facet A reflects the differences in lead and support roles. It is interesting to note that all three women were assessed to be the same on facet E which reflected that they had little personal authority with all three women giving away their authority to male characters. In terms of the facet of physical strength, the two support characters were only moderately strong, while Rachel, the female lead, was shown as a weak character. It is interesting to question whether this increasing weakness is a feature that allows Rachel to assume a leading role and to not threaten the positions of the leading men in the film. In a similar vein, facet C embodies judgements in relation to whether a female role embodies notions of a woman being a bad woman. Both of the support roles were indeed typified as bad women, as they portrayed femme fatales who attempted to subvert the male characters. Only the leading female character, Rachael, was not a femme fatale, rather she was cast as a "good woman" who is shown to be innocent. Our assessments of the characters on facet B indicated that both of the supporting female characters were portrayed as overtly sexual in appearance and Rachael was seen by us to be moderately sexualised. This would appear to be an important finding, as it suggests that all female characters in Blade Runner have their sexual appearance emphasised to some extent.

In conclusion, the profiles in Table 3.4 show that all women were depicted as having given away their personal authority to men and to have emphasised sexual appearance to some extent. The two support roles were both femme fatales or bad women with highly sexual appearance, while the female lead was weak and innocent but still moderately sexualised.

Conclusions

Science fiction movies of the past seem to echo the gender inequalities of society in their time.[1] More recently, science fiction movies are frequently thought of as presenting a glimpse into the future and as a hint of a future which they portray with progressive gender roles. However, when we look at *Blade Runner*, we have to disagree with this suggestion. In this chapter, our analyses have shown that female representations have failed to make progress in empowering women, when compared with earlier science fiction films and television programmes. Indeed, the film borrows heavily from the traditional femme fatale theme in order to create two female characters who lure and endanger the male protagonist. Therefore, *Blade Runner* continues to use common patriarchal storylines from previous works such as the femme fatale. The film also presents women as sexualised objects for the male gaze, with women being subservient both physically and psychologically to men. Finally, the portrayal of the female lead as a good woman is based upon a patriarchal standpoint. Although the cinematography in *Blade Runner* is worthy of praise, we have shown in our profile analyses that it should not be considered as a successful film in terms of the ways in which it represents gender roles. Blade Runner enhances patriarchal ideology by stressing female sexuality and making women the passive object of the male gaze. Additionally, female protagonists become disconnected body parts presented to the mass male audiences' eyes and simultaneously they are typically weak characters within the storyline. Blade Runner intensifies the past gender inequalities in the patriarchal system, but because the film was the first movie to include female Artificial Intelligence beings as protagonists, the film stands as an important model that deeply, but mistakenly, influenced the way in which later science fiction movies address gender inequality and female depiction. The hypersexualised images of women in the film contain a message regarding how women should behave and look which does little to fight against the perpetuation of society's gender stereotypes.

Note

1. It may be claimed that this is true of science fiction films from all eras, including the present.

References

Brammer, R. (2016) *Futuristic Femmes Fatales: The Android Women of Blade Runner, Screen Education*, Australian Teachers of Media Incorporated (ATOM). www.screeneducation.com.au

Des Roches, A. (2017) *Sexy Robots: A Perpetuation of Patriarchy*, San Luis Obispo: California Polytechnic State University.

Knapp, L.F., and Kulas, A.F. (2005) *Ridley Scott: Interviews*, Jackson, MS: University Press of Mississippi. ISBN: 157806726X, 978158067268.

Mulvey, L. (1975) Visual Pleasure and Narrative Cinema. Originally Published – Screen 16.3, Autumn 1975. https://doi.org/10.1093/screen/16.3.6

Redmond, S. (2008) *Studying Blade Runner*, Leighton: Auteur.

4   Ex Machina

Female Machines Versus Their Male Dictators

Introduction

Ex Machina is a 2015 science fiction film written and directed by Alex Garland. In the film, Caleb Smith (played by Domhnall Gleeson) is a programmer at a large and dominant search engine company, Blue Book. Nathan
Bateman (Oscar Isaac) is the company's CEO. Caleb won the chance to
spend a week at Nathan Bateman's private estate. While at Nathan's estate,
Caleb was the human component in a Turing test[1] undertaken to determine
the capabilities and consciousness of a female robot, Ava (played by Alicia
Vikander). While testing Ava's agency and having conversations with her,
Caleb became captivated by Ava's beauty and innocence. The deceptive
Ava pretended to love Caleb in order to manipulate him to set her free.
Caleb did not know that Ava was programmed to use him to aid in her
escape. During Caleb's visit, he discovered how cruelly Nathan treated
all his female robots, which triggered Caleb's distrust of Nathan's actual
purpose in making artificial intelligence robots (such as Ava). Looking
at Kyoko (Sonoya Mizuno), a mute Japanese female AI, Caleb began to
realise that Nathan designed these female androids only to serve his physical and sexual needs. Both Caleb and Kyoko helped Ava in her quest for
freedom. At the end, to achieve her purpose of escaping, Ava stabbed her
maker Nathan and imprisoned Caleb, and even Kyoko sacrifices herself in
order to aid Ava escape.

The structural design in the film builds up a distance between the
female cyborg, Ava, and the male computer tester, Caleb, and this distance articulates the noticeable disparity in the two characters' relative
power positions. When Caleb first met Ava, he was introduced to her living space – a glass room. The rectangular glass room creates depth within
which Ava's figure and posture become reflections being displayed on the
outside of the glass wall. Such a display enables the male computer programmer to monitor Ava's activities from every perspective. Furthermore,

DOI: 10.4324/9781003138419-4

the deliberate choice of glass surroundings suggests the construction of a laboratory design and emphasises the distance between the inside and the outside space. When Caleb and Ava converse in this surrounding, Ava becomes a female exhibit, a robotic exhibition or showpiece for Caleb, the human tester of her programme. Here, the audience begins to become aware of the explicit power of the male programmer when they see him sitting outside of the glass "lab" enjoying testing a female robot. In contradiction to the male position, the viewer also starts to perceive Ava's powerless and disadvantageous position, seeing her locked inside of the glass room. These aspects of the facility design are essential elements in the film's mise-en-scène which presents to the viewer the idea of unequal gender positions.

When the film is looked at in this way, it is reasonable to claim that disparities in gender representation have not been improved in *Ex Machina*. Female AI characters are still objects for the male gaze, while the male protagonists hold the extreme levels of power over female characters. Although *Ex Machina* (2015) was released 33 years after *Blade Runner* (1982), *Ex Machina* does not help demonstrate a positive progress in gender representation. In fact, *Ex Machina* represents a retrogression when compared to many sci-fi characters, such as Ripley in *Alien* (1979) and Sonny in *I, Robot* (2004). We discuss this later.

In the previous section, we have noted the storyline of *Ex Machina* and offered our brief reflections upon the way in which female characters are presented in the movie. In the following sections, we will use the declarative mapping sentence to "unpack" the roles of the two female characters.

Using Mapping Sentence to Analyse Female Characters

Facet Profiles of Female Characters

We commenced our writing about *Ex Machina* by offering a somewhat impressionistic account of how the two female robots are shown in the film. As in the previous two chapters, we will then break down and form the profiles of the characters in terms of the five facets of the declarative mapping sentence we are using in these analyses. These profiles are shown in Tables 4.1 and 4.2.

Having set out the profiles of our two female characters in Tables 4.1 and 4.2, we now begin to delve deeper into how each character is typified by each of the five facets in our analysis. We start with facet A of the actresses' role in the film.

Table 4.1 Facet Profile for Ava

Facet profile		Details
A1	• Role: • lead role	Ava is in the lead role and the female protagonist. Without her the movie could not exist. The entire film is about her trapping men in order to find a way to escape to the outside world.
• B3	• Sexual Appearance: • overly emphasised	Her sexual appearance is highly emphasised. Although Ava is an AI robot, she wears little clothing throughout the film. Her body shape is emphasised to show her having a perfect, slim female body. There are also some scenes which show her using her nude body to lure Caleb.
• C3	• Bad Woman: • femme fatale	She is portrayed as a femme fatale character. Ava used her beauty to lure and trap Caleb. She becomes a murderer who killed her maker, Nathan.
• D1	• Physical Strength: • strong	She is physically strong. Being a robot, her body is stronger and more perfect than a human body. Even though her arm is pulled off by Nathan she continues fighting and kills him.
• E1	• Personal Authority: • fully independent	Ava wants to escape to the outside world and uses men to achieve this goal. However, as she is a robot is she programmed or does she have independent choice? We claim that Ava appears to enjoy freedom and appeared to have a self-guided life.

Table 4.2 Facet Profile for Kyoko

Facet profile		Details
A2	Role: support role	The film is not telling Kyoko's story. She does not play the most important role.
• B3	Sexual Appearance: overly emphasised	Her sexual appearance is overtly emphasised. Most of the time she wears clothes that expose most of her body. There is a scene where she takes off her top.
• C3	Bad Woman: femme fatale	Her emotions are largely removed. Kyoko is a co-conspirator who helps Ava to murder and becomes a femme fatale character.
• D2	Physical Strength: Neutral	Her physical strength is not emphasised in the film.
• E3	Personal Authority: fully dependent	Fully dependent. She can neither speak nor make any decisions. She is Nathan's slave and has the sole purpose of serving him.

Profile Summary

In the aforementioned tables, we have presented the two female characters in the movie *Ex Machina* and we have evaluated along the five facets of our declarative mapping sentence. In Table 4.3, we offer a comparison of the facet profiles of Ava and Kyoko.

In Table 4.3, we can see that while Ava plays the lead role and Kyoko does not (facet A); both have sexual appearances which the director emphasises (facet B); and both characters are cast as femme fatales (facet C). However, where the characters differ is in their physical strength and personal authority (facets D and E, respectively). On these facets, Ava is physically strong and has personal authority, while Kyoko is assessed to be neutral in terms of her physical strength and have no personal authority. In the following sections, we provide more details about our assessment of the two characters of Ava and Kyoko and we will look more deeply into the meaning behind the two female characters and their stories.

Facet A: Female Role

Ava (A1 – Lead Role)

Ava occupies the lead role and is labelled A1 on the first facet, as she is the most important female protagonist. The entire film is about her trapping men in order to find her way to escape to the outside world. Her role is crucial to the movie that the whole movie is telling her story.

Kyoko (A2 – Support Role)

Kyoko plays a supporting female role, so we rated her as A2 on this facet. We made this decision, as her part is not as important as Ava to the plot. The film is not her story. Without her, the story would still exist, although it would be very different. Nevertheless, her role still maintains significance and has much to say about gender standards in the film.

Table 4.3 Comparison of Profiles for Three Female Characters

Character	Facet A	Facet B	Facet C	Facet D	Facet E
Ava	A1	B3	C3	D1	E1
Kyoko	A2	B3	C3	D2	E3

Facet B: Sexual Appearance

Ava (B3 – Overly Emphasised)

The director Alex Garland makes an argument that the females are represented in *Ex Machina* in a genderless manner. However, we believe that this is highly questionable and problematic claim. While being a robot, Ava is also a female, and her sexual appearance is overtly emphasised. Thus, we rate Ava as a B3.

Garland insists that Ava is an androgynous cyborg and refuses to categorise Ava as a female robot. In an interview with Angela Watercutter (2015) for Wired called "*Ex Machina* Has a Serious Fembot Problem," Garland said, Ava isn't a woman and claims that she is literally genderless. He continues to emphasise that the attributes that would define male and female gender are lacking in Ava, except in external terms. Watercutter also states that she is unsure whether consciousness even has a gender. The veracity of this declaration is highly questionable, because, first and foremost, referring Ava as a "she" has already expressed her role as a female, and throughout the film, she uses her female body in a seductive manner.

Moreover, Garland states that Ava's external appearance is the only thing that defines her gender, but she lacks internal characteristics that would determine her to be either a man or a woman. We do not agree with his claim that the external appearance means nothing about gender or sexuality, and argue that Ava's external body is the evidence of her feminity. Ava is a woman and we believe that the audience would definitely deem Ava as a woman from the first sight to the last. When Ava appears to on screen for the first time, we see Ava's body shape, her skull, arms, waist and legs which appear to be covered in transparent mesh-like material disclosing her interior skeleton structure. Her muscles are metal and the blue and yellow light in her abdominal part is her blood. Initially, she is in a mechanical form. However, as Ava comes closer, her feminine traits become visible. Although the transparent aspects seem genderless, the most important body parts (breasts, pubic area and buttocks) for identifying the sex of the person are covered in grey metal fibre, which reveals her female sexuality. The transparent parts in her technological body actually highlight her female, sexual areas. These central feminine features clearly define Ava's gender as a woman.

As Ashlyn Des Roches points out,

> If the robot is shown with two clearly defined breasts (although lacking nipples and areola), as well as two protruding hip bones pointing down to meet at the pubic union, just as a woman's body structure often

presents, then one might be led to the assumption that this "androgynous" machine is typically what one may refer to as "female."

(p. 25)

Audiences would never doubt Ava's feminine status, and they would probably agree that she is pretty and fits the modern beauty standards. Her slender
body shape and skinny belly (looking like a corset) form a sense of softness
and fragility, which conforms with conventional female attributes. As Cath-
erine Constable (2018) points out "Ava is youthful and very slender – the
insubstantial shaping the glass corset creating a new technological size 0"
(Constable, 2018, p. 292). Hence, Ava is by no means genderless. The mass
audience will not be fooled by the director's decisions.

Women's sexuality is highly emphasised and displayed in this film for
men to look at. Laura Mulvey says,

> In a world ordered by sexual imbalance, pleasure in looking has been
> split between active/male and passive/female. . . . In their traditional
> exhibitionist role, women are simultaneously looked at and displayed,
> with their appearance coded for strong visual and erotic impact.

(Mulvey, 1975)

When Ava tried to surprise Caleb by dressing herself up, she was preparing to be seen through the male gaze, Caleb's gaze. Ava told Caleb to close
his eyes and wait for her, and she then went to her wardrobe choosing a wig
and clothes. Ava touched Jean Seberg-esque's poster on the wall and tried
to imitate her style, because Jean's picture is a photo-fit based on Caleb's
pornography profile. Ava ultimately came back to Caleb with an innocent
and youthful look: a pixie cut hairstyle, a blue-purple patterned dress, a
light blue cardigan and a pair of soft white woollen stockings. After asking
Caleb "How do I look?," Ava turned around to display herself to Caleb as
if she was an object. Caleb's uncomfortable reaction implies the satisfac-
tion he gained from looking and his attraction to Ava. When Ava was getting undressed, Caleb was secretly peeping through the monitoring camera.
Under the shadow and the gloomy lighting, Ava slowly and softly took off
her stockings and dress. The setting of the dressing scene foreshadows the
undressed scene. Ava then again wore no clothes on her body as she did
at the beginning of the film, but her metal body now generates a sense of
nudity that is different from the beginning. After seeing Ava's striptease,
Caleb would no longer visualise Ava simply as a robot, but he was only able
to see her as a sexualised object. As with Caleb, the audience will start to
see Ava as a complete woman.

Kyoko (B3 – Overly Emphasised)

Kyoko is rated as B3, because her sexuality is overtly emphasised in the movie. Men in the movie decide how the women should be and look. Nathan controls all his fembots and these fembots are there to satisfy Nathan's sexual desires. Kyoko is in a very similar fashion to Pris, a pleasure doll in *Blade Runner*. Kyoko's presence in the film is all about her sexuality.

When Caleb tried to find Nathan, he met Kyoko in Nathan's room, so he asked Kyoko where Nathan was. At this moment, Kyoko had an erotic appearance with her legs fully exposed as she had no pants on wearing only a light-weight shirt with no bra. The mute android could not understand a single word he said, but she only thought he was coming to her for sex. She looked at him and tried to unbutton her top. Kyoko was programmed to believe that the only thing men would want or need from her was sex. Additionally, making Kyoko a mute robot emphasises her sexual purpose and detaches her participation from any communication. The fembots were programmed to be how Nathan wanted them to be and behave. Nathan programmed all fembots to be slaves and unquestioning sexual partners. In a sense, the film puts women in an even lower position than they were in earlier aged movies and panders to a patriarchal ideology instead of challenging it.

Facet C: Bad Woman

Ava (C3 – Femme Fatale)

In our analyses, we rated Ava as C3 on facet C, because she portrays what is obviously a femme fatale character. The filmic story in *Ex Machina* is about a robot using sexuality to manipulate male programmers in order to escape to the outside world. Ava as a femme fatale character pursued her journey to freedom by luring and seducing Caleb to fall in love with her. She then used Caleb's emotion towards her to manipulate him and set a trap for Caleb to step in, which resulted in Caleb being locked up in the facility. To reach her ultimate goal of freedom, Ava stabbed and killed Nathan.

While Ava is being strong in the sense that she killed and defeated Nathan, in this femme fatale storyline, Ava is not a good powerful woman but a lying murderer which does not characterise strength. We argue that her success of pursuing the dream of escaping into the real world is not at all feminist, as it is achieved through immorality. Therefore, by drawing from the classic femme fatale plot, the film does not help break the misogynous standpoint that strong women represent a danger to men.

Kyoko (C3 – Femme Fatale)

As with the character Ava, we rated Kyoko as C3 on this facet. At the beginning of the film, Kyoko's character is portrayed as neither good nor evil. Indeed, Kyoko is an enticing fembot, but her character is one of a "Spock-like" female robot, with her emotions being almost entirely removed. However, at the very end of the film, we are shown that Kyoko may indeed have emotions. She was the accomplice that helped Ava to escape and kill Nathan, and as such she became a femme fatale.

Facet D: Physical Strength

Ava (D1 – Strong)

On the fourth facet, we rated Ava as D1, since she is shown as being physically strong. Being a female robot, her body is stronger and more perfect than a human body and even stronger than men. At the end of the film, Ava fought Nathan. Although Ava's arm was torn off by Nathan during the fight, she was not affected by the loss of her arm and she used her strength to beat Nathan.

Kyoko (D2 – Neutral)

Unlike Ava's rating, we rate Kyoko's physical strength as neutral. Her physical strength is not emphasised in the film, but she is definitely not portrayed as a strong character in the way that Ava is. Indeed, Nathan intentionally made Kyoko weaker than Ava and used Kyoko as a maid instead of as a fighter. Thus, Kyoko simply listened to Nathan instead of fighting back.

Facet E: Personal Authority

Ava (E1 – Fully Independent)

On the fifth and final facet, Ava is rated E1, because she is fully independent when deciding her own actions. Ava wanted to escape to the outside world and used men to achieve her goal. However, it may be claimed that she is a robot whose mind is made up by Nathan, her male maker. On this understanding, Ava is innocent as she is just a programmed machine and her escape is not indicative of her own free will. However, we tend to disagree with this point of view that Ava has none of her own thoughts. This is because, at the end of the film, Ava finally escapes and appears to enjoy her freedom. However, if she is only a product of her programming and her actions are only due to programs, then she will not have further desires when she is in the outside world. Also in this sense, she needs to be programmed again to have feelings in the real society. However, when Ava finally went to the outside, she was not confused about what she needed to do next, but she was obviously really happy to explore things based on her own mind. Thus, we believe this indicates that Ava had her own ideas and that she consciously experiences the world.

Kyoko (E3 – Fully Dependent)

Kyoko was fully dependent on Nathan, so we rated her as E3. Her gender position in *Ex Machina* conforms to the existing stereotypes that women occupy a lower social position than men. Nathan, the female robot creator, symbolises men's controlling status over women, and women's powerlessness in relation to men. The unspoken patriarchal dominance becomes extremely apparent when considering the interaction between Nathan and his female robots. Nathan used Kyoko as a server. The first time Kyoko appeared in the film is when Caleb and Nathan were having dinner together. From a long shot cutting to a medium shot, Kyoko held dishes to serve at the men's table. Kyoko accidently spilt wine over Caleb which provoked an immediate angry reaction from him. When Kyoko knelt down to clean the mess up, Nathan said to Caleb, "you are wasting your time talking to her. She doesn't understand English. Just give her the napkin." For Nathan, Kyoko occupies a slave-like role and she should unquestioningly serve him and his guest. Conversely, for Kyoko, Nathan is like a God and upon whom Kyoko is fully dependent on for decision making, and without whom, her existence has no purpose. Nathan made Kyoko a mute AI because he did not want to waste his time communicating with her. In his mind, serving, cleaning and cooking are the female robot's only functions.

Conclusion

During the South by Southwest Festival, a Tinder (a geosocial networking and online dating app) profile for the character of Ava was created, and Ava was matched with other Tinder profiles. This marketing strategy for the movie is quite interesting and also effective to target younger audiences. However, this marketing tool reinforces the film's social ideology that women are made to find a male mate and to be placed on exhibition being scrutinised at by men. In *Ex Machina*, gender positions follow binary and patriarchal gender standards. Women are in a lower social and personal position, and men hold the power to decide what women should be like. This film again borrows the femme fatale theme from the classic noir films and crafts a story of a heroine trapping heroes in order to gain her freedom. This film intensifies patriarchal ideology by perpetuating a patriarchal femme fatale storyline. Thus, even though the film's visual design is so proficient that it won Academy Award for Best Visual Effects, the film should not be uncritically categorised as a success due to the obvious polarisation of male and female representations in the movie. To put it simply, female roles are downplayed and negatively portrayed through a pair of patriarchal eyes in *Ex Machina*.

Accordingly, *Ex Machina* perpetuates gender stereotypes by over-sexualising female robots and reducing them into sexual products for men's needs. Even though Ava's purpose is to refuse the patriarchal dominance, her revenge and poor morality trigger us to think whether this kind of act really solves gender problems: We suggest that it does not. Ava's character certainly does not help improve gender equality, since the femme fatale theme signifies and intensifies a misogynous perspective.

At the end of the film, we are left with a question: what will happen after the film's ending scene, after Ava finally successfully arrives in the outside world? When Ava sees all the human beings looking similar to her on the outside but different from her on the inside, what will she do? Have her feeling and perception of human beings already been shaped by Nathan's cruelty? If this is so, she will forever consider human beings as threat, and then we are asked to question what her response to this outlook to be? In order to achieve her goals, Ava will probably continue to act as a femme fatale manipulating and murdering more men. If this is the case, men will fear women due to women's potential ability to seduce and harm them. This is likely to do little to improve the representation of women on screen and to deepen gender conflicts and gender stereotypes, which in a sense further traps females as passive objects.

Note

1 Named after Alan Turing, the Turing test (1950) is a test that Turing believed a machine would be able to perform such a test (which he called an imitation game) in a manner that it could not be distinguished from human beings performing the same task. In the test a machine is observed having a conversation with a human. The observer knows that there is both a human and being and a machine in the dyad and the conversation takes place through text and not verbally. The machine passes the test if the observer cannot differentiate between the two participants based upon the text conversation. There are several versions of the test.

References

Constable, C. (2018) Surfaces of Science Fiction: Enacting Gender and "Humanness" in Ex Machina, *Film-Philosophy*, 22(2).

Des Roches, A. (2017) *Sexy Robots: A Perpetuation of Patriarchy*, San Luis Obispo: California Polytechnic State University. https://digitalcommons.calpoly.edu/comssp/220

Mulvey, L. (1975) Visual Pleasure and Narrative Cinema. Originally Published – Screen 16.3, Autumn 1975. https://doi.org/10.1093/screen/16.3.6

Turing, A. (1950) Computing, Machinery and Intelligence, *Mind*, LIX(236), 433–460, https://doi.org/10.1093/mind/LIX.236.433, ISSN 0026–4423.

Watercutter, A. (2015) Ex Machina Has a Serious Fembot Problem, *Wired*, www.wired.com/2015/04/ex-machina-turing-bechdel-test/

5 Star Trek

Discovery – "The Vulcan Hello": A Utopian Universe

Introduction

Created by Bryan Fuller and Alex Kurtzman, *Star Trek: Discovery* is the seventh series in the *Star Trek* franchise. When it appeared on screens, *the Discovery series* was conceived as a new television programme and it was not released on a traditional television broadcast network. Instead, it was launched, in 2017, on CBS All Access. The season's first episode "The Vulcan Hello" was written by Akiva Goldsman and Bryan Fuller and directed by David Semel. The show starring two women of colour, an African American officer and an Asian American leader, may in many ways be seen to be more advanced in its portrayal of women than other science fiction stories, such as *Star Wars: The Force Awakens* (2015) and *Arrival* (2016), both of which contain white females in central roles. The story of *Discovery*, which is set a decade before the time of the original *Star Trek*, shows the initiation of the "cold war" between the Federation and Klingon forces. When the first episode aired on CBS, the show was viewed by over nine million people and received positive reviews from critics.

Discovery starts its story with Captain Philippa Georgiou (Michelle Yeoh) leading the spaceship U.S.S. Shenzhou and Michael Burnham (Sonequa Martin-Green) serving as the First Officer/Commander. Michael encounters and kills a Klingon while she is exploring an unrecognised starship. Michael lost consciousness during this time but managed to successfully transferred back to the Shenzhou. When she woke up, she found herself to be injured and receiving treatment in a medical care room. Abandoning her treatment, Michael rushes to tell Captain Philippa the danger they might have encountered. The crew of the starship refuse to believe that Michael had encountered a Klingon, but Captain Philippa believes Michael and sends a message to the Klingon ship in an attempt to achieve reconciliation. However, Michael's resentment towards Klingons, which is based upon memories of her experiences with them, impels her to oppose Captain Philippa's

DOI: 10.4324/9781003138419-5

decision about the necessary steps that need to be taken to engage with the Klingons. Michael later knocks Philippa out and gives a fake order to the crew. Philippa eventually wakes and rescinds Michael's order.

The Original Series of Star Trek simply made gender diversity visible on screen but missed many opportunities of character development. Nevertheless, the *Discovery* series has engaged in a deeper representation of its female characters in that it casts "several prominent and important women whose presence suggests not just the visibility of female astronauts but a depth and complexity missing from earlier Star Trek programmes" (Keeler, 2019, p. 136). Comparing this series with the very first episode of the Star Trek franchise, "The Man Trap," that we reviewed in an earlier chapter, it is obvious that *Discovery* has really moved on to a whole new level where women leaders are neither sexual objects nor useless adjuncts. The *Discovery* Series has totally changed the gender and racial representation in science fiction. Women can themselves now lead a spaceship and give orders to both women and men. The relationships between women and collaborations between different genders and races, in this series, are complex and have been framed within a whole new focus.

Using Mapping Sentences to Analyse Female Characters

Facet Profiles of Female Characters

During the following section, we will provide a review of the two female characters, Michael Burnham and Captain Philippa Georgiou, together, since they have exactly the same facet profiles. Their similarities will be analysed by using each facet element (from facets A to E). Nonetheless, there are some differences between the characters and they will be discussed in the following paragraphs.

Table 5.1 Facet Profile for Michael Burnham

Facet profile		Details
A1	• Role: • lead role	She is the most important character in the episode.
		She has her own story to tell.
		She engages in explorations and risks.
• B1	• Sexual Appearance: • not emphasised	Her sexual appearance is not emphasised.
		Her costume does not draw attention but serves the purpose of helping her actively participate in activities rather than displaying her sexuality or beauty.

Facet profile		Details
• C1	Bad Woman: not bad	She is portrayed as a strong rather than a bad woman.
• D1	• Physical Strength: • strong	She is shown as physical strong.
		She does not hesitate to entre dangerous situations.
		She protects herself and fights her enemies.
		She does not need men to protect her.
• E1	• Personal Authority: • fully independent	She is fully independent.
		She decides and acts for herself.
		She is brave in the face of challenges.

Table 5.2 Facet Profile for Captain Philippa Georgiou

Facet profile		Details
A1	Role: lead role	She is also one of the show's most essential characters.
		She is the leader of the ship, U.S.S. Shenzhou.
		She makes decisions for the ship.
• B1	Sexual Appearance: not emphasised	Her sexual appearance is not emphasised.
• C1	Bad Woman: not bad	She is portrayed as a strong and not a bad woman.
• D1	Physical Strength: Strong	She is shown as physical strong.
		She does not hesitate to entre dangerous situations.
		She protects herself and fights her enemies.
		She does not need men to protect her.
• E1	Personal Authority: fully independent	She is fully independent.
		When there are threats to the ship, she takes the lead and is not afraid of making decisions.

Table 5.3 Comparison of Profiles for Three Female Characters

Character	Facet A	Facet B	Facet C	Facet D	Facet E
Michael Burnham	A1	B1	C1	D1	E1
Captain Philippa Georgiou	A1	B1	C1	D1	E1

Profile Summary

Facet A: Female Role

Michael Burnham (A1 – Lead Role) and Captain Philippa
Georgiou (A1 – Lead Role)

In the *Discovery* series, both the characters of Michael and Philippa are A1, lead roles. They both are essential in the narratives in the story. They occupy the cardinal roles in the episode and are central to the episode's plot. The characters of Michael and Philippa are self-motivated and self-guided, as they explore outer space and they engage in dangerous storylines. Indeed, in this episode, Michael is chosen to be the first person to undertake a dangerous mission.

The females lead characters are not just sidekicks in this show, but they are leaders of the spaceship. They are excluded neither from any type of job or activity they engage in nor from being leaders; leaders that possess admirable important and commendable leadership abilities. These characters are women leaders with talents, skills and abilities. They are powerful women who demonstrate strong leadership.

Facet B: Sexual Appearance

Michael Burnham (B1 – Not Emphasised) Captain Philippa
Georgiou (B1 – Not Emphasised)

Both Michael and Philippa are rated as B1 on this facet element. In the *Discovery* series, the costumes of Michael Burnham and Captain Philippa Georgiou are refutations of female objectification, demonstrating an evolution in the equality of gender depiction. Their costumes do not emphasise female sexuality but are designed to allow the characters to fulfil their purposes and to freely engage in challenging and dangerous activities. This is very different from the 1960s' Star Trek episodes which were restrictive in their portrayal of female abilities and it reflects how more recent television programmes and films offer different types of gender representations. Female characters are not only included in the episodes of Star Trek in order that they may be looked at by the mass male audience, but they have important stories of their own to tell. According to Andres (2013), "the evolution of the female officers' uniforms from feminized dressed to androgynous clothing over the development of the series (reflects) the change of gender roles in contemporary American society" (Andres, 2013, p. 639). From wearing miniskirts which exposed all of the characters' legs to dressing in practical and futuristic military style attire, female characters no longer need to be the objects of the male gaze due to their having sexy clothing, but rather they are transformed into significant individuals who wear suitable costumes for their jobs and duties. Women no longer rely on men or men's gaze to be present in the story, as they have finally become autonomous individuals with their own stories. In "The Vulcan Hello," Michael and Philippa, as the primary protagonists, did not wear different or eye-catching costumes. Instead, when they are on Shenzhou, Michael and Philippa dressed in navy unisex space jump-suits, just the same as the other crewmen. In this sense, the show does not try to emphasise Michael and Philippa's sexuality, but it tries to convey that both female characters do not need to have their sexualised presence emphasised through their costumes. Ultimately, this show pushes audiences to focus on female characters' personal stories instead of their sexuality and the transformation of costumes from the original Star Trek to the Discovery series perhaps reflects a progress in gender equality in society today.

Not only costumes but also the whole looks of actresses empower female roles. It is clear that female characters do not need to enhance their feminine faces or expose their female body for the audiences' attention. However, the female characters' strong personalities and the quality of their acting are intriguing enough to attract viewers. It should, however, be mentioned that the actresses in Discovery are still portrayed in an attractive manner, but that this is a look which embodies female power. It is also of interest to note that the female characters' makeup is of a type that is unique and memorable rather than emphasising their sexiness. Michelle Yeoh, who stars as Captain Philippa, is not a young girl but an elder Asian lady. However, she is beautiful, with her beauty not just simply emphasised in her makeup, hair or clothes but in her personality and her energy. She is elegant and produces a sense of graceful glamour and dignified mystery. Furthermore, the African American Commander Michael, who has clean-cut short hair, is also not just a pretty image. Michael was injured and her face was burned, but the character does not care about this at all. When she was injured, all she cared about was her responsibility to protect her crew, which causes her to refuse treatment for her injuries and to rush to Captain Philippe in order to warn her of the danger from the Klingons. Michael's face and her own beauty are not the most important thing to her, with her care for the ship and the crew are being crucial.

Facet C: Bad Woman

Michael Burnham (C1 – Not Bad) Captain Philippa Georgiou
(C1 – Not Bad)

Both Michael and Philippa are not portrayed as a bad woman but as women who are strong and brave and who make decisions for the good of their ship and colleagues. Michael is courageous and risks herself when she realises the danger to the starship Shenzhou. Philippa is decisive and leads the crew when they encountered the Klingons.

Facet D: Physical Strength

Michael Burnham (D1 – Strong) Captain Philippa
Georgiou (D1 – Strong)

Both Michael and Philippa are categorised as D1, because they are not afraid of confrontation and participating in risky events or fighting with aggressive enemies and it is clear that *Discovery* tries to portray Michael and Philippa as physically strong characters. For instance, when the Shenzhou encounters the unrecognised ship, officer Michael decides to further explore the ship. Even though she knows that this might be a personal risk for her, she is willing to take the opportunity to complete the task of identifying the unknown ship. Furthermore, when she encounters an unknown creature, she does not run away from this. As her realisation grows that the creature in front of her is a Klingon, her first reaction is to communicate with it. "I'm Commander Burnham of the United Federation of . . ."; however, before she finished speaking, she is attacked by the creature requiring her to fight and stab the creature. She did not call for help or run away, but she stood her ground and fought back using her own physical strength.

Facet E: Personal Authority

Michael Burnham (E1 – Fully Independent) Captain Philippa
Georgiou (E1 – Fully Independent)

We rated Michael and Philippa as E1, because they make their own decisions and determine their own actions. This is demonstrated in very many scenes, such as when Michael and Philippa fly the Shenzhou and encounter an unrecognised ship, officer Michael asks to explore the ship while Captain Philippa agrees. In this, as in many other scenes, both Michael and Philippa are decisive leaders who rely upon their own judgement.

Discovery does not just focus on manifesting female independence but develops gender equality further by showing harmonious collaborations between women and men. When Michael commenced her expedition to find the identity of the unrecognised ship, all crewmen, both women and men, worked together and communicated with Michael. This is very different from *The Original Series* which had a lack of female leadership, plot lines and collaborations among genders: *Discovery* demonstrates both. Help, trust and collaboration between characters are all portrayed in the show.

The depiction of the relationship between women is a major component in the *Discovery* series, and instead of female characters competing with each other over the attentions of men, female characters help and collaborate with each other in meaningful ways and tasks. "People always think you put two women in the same place and they compete with each other," says Yeoh, the actress who plays Captain Philippa, "'She's older, so she's going to be jealous of the young one. They're going to fight over a man.' It's all absolutely not true, and it's a silly thing to encourage" (Dockterman, 2017, p. 60). The show also stresses the trust between two female leading roles. As we noted earlier, when Michael found a Klingon on the starship, other crew members did not believe her, but Captain Philippa trusted Michael's words. However, when the two women disagree with each other, Michael shows that she does not fear objecting to an authority figure. For example, Michael's memories of Klingons drive her to oppose Captain Philippa's decision about what steps to be taken to engage with the Klingons, resulting in her knocking Philippa out and giving fake order to the crew.

In *Discovery*, female characters are finally allowed to have complex relationships with each other and these take many forms. When compared to the original *Star Trek*'s rare meaningful female interactions, *Discovery* offers chances for women to tell their own complicated stories.

Conclusion

The narratives in films and the outside world are often closely linked and interact with each other. Gender inequalities in film stories are shaped by the social norms from the real world. Characters in science fiction movies can be understood as projections of gender representations of the society within which the film or programme was made. However, filmmaking also has a great potential to improve the representation of issues associated with social justice in our contemporary daily lives. *Star Trek: Discovery* has become a successful television series and this success demonstrates that much progress has been made in the way in which race and gender are portrayed in television shows and movies. *Discovery* not only allows gender diversity to be visible, it also permits us to see the missing points in *The Original Star*

Trek's gender representation. Rather than just placing the female character on the screen, as was the case in *Star Trek: The Original Series*, *Discovery* goes far beyond the surface and delves deeply into female character developments and offers women complex identities and back stories. In *Discovery*, female roles are no inept sidekicks, but instead women in this show take a commanding position in the narrative. It is also worth noting that the show contains male roles that are of equal importance to the female roles and who also collaborate with these female characters.

In conclusion, *Star Trek: Discovery* has come a long way from the earlier *Star Trek* series and offers programmes which place the roles of women centrally within its plots. In comparison, the female characters in the original *Star Trek* series are present but their characters are not complex, developed or central to the narrative. *Discovery* is perhaps a starting point for a utopian society where women can be powerful as men. However, perhaps the most appealing aspect of *Discovery* is the harmonious interpersonal relationship between men and women which suggests and encourages gender equality with meaningful interactions. Ultimately, *Discovery* suggests that gender issues may no longer be unsurmountable problems as the *Discovery* series provides us with a palette with which to paint a form of a utopian future with equality. To conclude, in contrast to *Star Trek: The Original Series*, *Star Trek: Discovery* presents a situation on-board the spaceship in which inspired female roles challenge patriarchal conceptions through powerful leadership and collaborative team works.

References

Andres, K. (2013) Fashion's Final Frontier: The Correlation of Gender Roles and Fashion in Star Trek, *Culture Unbound*, 5, 642, Linkoping University Electronic Press.

Dockterman, E. (2017) In a Quantum Leap, Star Trek Becomes a Female Enterprise, *Time Off*, 59–60.

Keeler, A. (2019) Visible/Invisible: Female Astronauts and Technology in Star Trek: Discovery and National Geographic's Mars, *Liverpool University Press, Science Fiction Film and Television*, 12(1), 136.

6 Conclusion

Synthesis of Findings

The Representation of Women in Science Fiction Film and TV

Gender and gender representation are central topics within films and television, with depictions typically being unequal between men and women across a variety of dimensions. As part of our exploration, we also consider the cultural and political contexts in which films are made and the potential impacts of such factors on gender representation. When movies were first developed, they were often about escapism and fantasy. Dating back to the earliest of films, such as Fritz Lang's Metropolis (1927), such dream-like worlds were regularly speculative and futuristic in their nature. Making a science fiction film presented the auteur with many imaginative possibilities that were not available to other forms of creativity such as stage and written media. For example, the filmmaker was able to fashion and capture their ideas for later alterations in the darkroom. Special effects became an ever-present component of such films which set about creating alternate possibilities both on earth and within and outside of our own solar system. With all of the opportunities that were available to the science fiction movie maker to create utopias, questions may be asked as to the extent women were portrayed in ways which extended and enriched their lives as individuals and their social roles. However, the chance to offer women an imaginary expansion to their roles in society was one that was not typically seized and it is very common practice for filmmakers to resort to the development of female characters that represent women as rooted in their contemporary positions or, for example, as the evil and cliched temptress.

One common way of portraying women in written fiction is as a perilous woman or femme fatale who lures men from their true destiny through temptation. This role is also present in science fiction and has been a major recurrent theme. The garden of Eden may seem an incongruous location to include in a book that is about science fiction television shows and cinema.

DOI: 10.4324/9781003138419-6

However, this mythical location is an early example of how women have been rendered as temptresses and as creatures that bring about the ruination of a man. In the story of Adam and Eve, we see Adam being beguiled by Eve who goads him into eating an apple from the tree of knowledge that God has prohibited him to eat from. Many other mythical female beings have lured men to their peril, and death with such females is present in Greek mythology. For example, the sirens were female creatures who enticed sailors with their evocative songs and music until the sailors were drawn to sail too close to the rocks that were around their island causing their boats to be wrecked. At many times in history, Sirens have been employed as a symbol of the dangerous temptation that women possess and the power they have over men. This is perhaps epitomised by Cornelius a Lapide who stated that a woman's glance could cause a man to die, that she is able to enchant men with her voice, and that her beauty is able to remove reason from men and to bring about death and destruction (Longworth and Tice, 1945). There are examples of similar perilous mystical female characters from other cultures. As an illustration, in Denmark, such female creatures exist in a medieval ballad called Elvehoj (Jonsson et al., 1994). Mermaids were created and performed in a similar manner to the Sirens, and in Hindu myths, Mohini enchants a variety of male characters. Other mythical historical perilous women include: Circe, Cleopatra, Clytemnestra, Daji, Delilah, Jezebel, Lesbos, Lilith, Medea, Messalina and Salome (Jung, 1968). I could continue to list the occurrences of women who have been cast in this role over the last 2,000 years. This is especially true in the fine arts, plays, opera and literature. However, this is beyond the scope of the present writing.

Nevertheless, it is worth noting that the dangerous temptress archetype has been found in the guise of the femme fatale, vamp or maneater. Femme fatales are usually cast in the role of villains (Doane, 1991). It is of particular interest in the context of the present book that femme fatale characters are often to be found in American movies and in film noir, gangster movies and even in James Bond (Manion and Ursini, 2009; Scaraffia, 2009). In direct reference to the first media offering we reviewed, *Star Trek – The Man Trap*, the femme fatale is depicted as a vampire who draws the life force from her male victims.

The femme fatale is only one of the ways in which women have been cast and depicted in creative and artistic forms of representation. We have concentrated a little time on the so called vamp as the stereotype is so pervasive as to warrant inclusion in our research. Another reason for our inclusion of the bad woman, femme fatale, temptress or vamp cliche in this discussion is because it saddens us that this hackneyed representation of women is still present in science fiction films. It appears to us that science fiction is in a unique position to offer inspirational or cautionary visions of positive and negative possibilities and future options. We seem to have little difficulty presenting such visions in terms of technological promises, but the genre has often shied away from breaking free from restrictive stereotypes and has kept female representation trapped within these, perhaps for commercial reasons and in an attempt to attract and appeal to a largely male audience.

Our Research

In this book, we have explored gender representations of specific female characters in two television programmes: *Star Trek: The Original Series* and *Star Trek: Discovery*, and in two movies: *Blade Runner* and *Ex Machina*. We have viewed and appraised these through critical thinking and through a critical lens of online and offline research. We have also performed analyses of characters through the development of declarative mapping sentence profiles. By looking deeply at all the main female protagonists in these four television and film pieces, we have realised and demonstrated the complexity of gender portrayals present in these programmes and films. From the earliest production we reviewed, "The Man Trap" through to the most contemporary, "The Vulcan Hello," we unlocked complexities in the gender representations and the possibilities of gender equality through repeatedly re-watching the pieces, a process which has taken several months.

In order to attempt to understand how women were shown in the pieces we viewed and to hint at solutions to improve gender representations, we focused our critical analyses upon characters' personalities, abilities and activities, appearances, costumes, interactions and dialogues. We noted and analysed the common themes in the four pieces which included: femme fatale heroines; hypersexualisation and objectification of women for the male gaze; unimportant and useless female sidekick characters; lack of interactions between female characters. Our analyses suggested a close relationship between the fictional stories we considered and the real world and between narratives and social norms, rather than offering women the chance of advancement in their roles. When we looked at the original *Star Trek*, we developed an extremely critical view of how women were presented, as they were shown as having little autonomy and not offering a positive model for women. However, by the time we reached the most contemporary of the media we considered, the ways in which women were portrayed has changed and women were now autonomous, strong and did not depend on their looks or on support from men. Accordingly, we changed our opinion of how women were represented from being critical of the female roles into acknowledging the positive role and influence of the show.

To illustrate this, in the first Star Trek episode, Nichelle Nichols plays the role of Lieutenant Uhura. When the character is placed within the historical context of the 1960s, the role takes on a significance. Nichelle Nichols not only empowered gender and racial minorities but also became an inspirational actress for both females and African Americans. Her frequent presence in the first episode of the original *Star Trek* emboldens and enables the possibility of gender and racial diversity in American television and film industry and even in a wider society. Subsequent to this initial Star Trek episode in 1966, and the seminal placement of an African American female on the screen, the *Star Trek* series has pushed forward gender equality. For example, in 1995, actress Kate Mulgrew starred in the role of Kathryn Janeway, the first female captain in *Star Trek: Voyager*. However, it should be noted that it was only this most recent shows from the *Discovery* series that had broken free from some of the limiting female stereotypes.

The femme fatale theme is still a persistent and commonly used trope around which plots have been, and still are, developed. Those films may be rooted within males' fear of powerful or beautiful women who are able to trap and lure men to obtain what they want and within men's fear that they are helpless when faced with a beautiful and powerful woman. When used in movies, this theme results in the production of a woman cast through patriarchal eyes as an immoral devil and thus generates and perpetuates misogynous ideas towards women. It is obvious that such a portrayal of women in science fiction, which was once commonplace, is to some extent disappearing. The first episode of *Star Trek: The Original Series* had a femme fatale female character as its main protagonist, but by the time we get to *Star Trek Discovery*, women are portrayed as powerful in their own right and not as a threat to masculine dominance and men's insecurities. To present a rough indication of how there has been a change in the depiction of women in science fiction moving media, Table 6.1 illustrates this point.

In our assessments of the portrayal of women, a rating of 1 is the most positive rating that we gave. A rating of 3 was the most negative. Obviously, a rating of 2 fell midway between these two points. In Table 6.1, we have included the numerical ratings for each woman in all four films on all the five facets upon which we rated their roles. We have, for facets 2–5, shaded the ratings from: unshaded (1); medium shade (2); darkly shaded (3). The first facet indicated whether the role was lead or support and we have shaded darkly lead roles (1) and unshaded support roles (2). It is apparent that there is a progression from light to dark on all five facets representing a positive progression in terms of women's representation on all assessment criteria. In the indices column is presented the proportion of ratings that were in some way positive (1 and 2) for all facets. Again, this demonstrates the positive progression in women's roles. The table also demonstrates that the

Table 6.1 Our Ratings of All Four Female Characters in All Four Productions

Character	Facet A	Facet B	Facet C	Facet D	Facet E	Indices
Nancy Crater	1	3	3	3	3	.25
Nyoto Uhura	2	3	1	3	3	
Pris	2	3	3	2	3	.33
Zhora	2	3	3	2	3	
Rachel	1	2	1	3	3	
Ava	1	3	3	1	1	.40
Kyoko	2	3	3	2	3	
Michael Burnham	1	1	1	1	1	1.0
Captain Philla Georgiou	1	1	1	1	1	

oldest and most recent productions are poles apart from each other and that significant changes have been made on all criteria. However, the two films from periods between the two extremes demonstrate that advancement was not simple as changes appeared to happen in an apparently random manner.

We believe that *Star Trek: The Original Series* had a positive influence in terms of gender equality, but the show still needed to place more attention upon the character development of the women. *Blade Runner* and *Ex Machina* both contain negative female representations that perpetuate the patriarchal gaze and standpoint. However, both the femme fatale and the sexualisation of women disappeared in *Discovery*, while female leadership and meaningful interactions for female characters came to the fore. Thus, *Star Trek Discovery* represents significant progress in the portrayal of women in science fiction and leads to the hope that this may represent a future vision of greater gender equality. In *Discovery*, the intersection of race and gender is positive. *When commenting about her role as in the programme, Star Trek's* first African American leading actor, Martin-Green says:

> I'm a black woman raised in the South, so that's something that I have always had an unfortunate understanding of. But on the flip side, it was surprising, because to say that you love Star Trek but you're upset about diversity on the show is completely antithetical.
>
> (Dockterman, 2017, pp. 59–60)

On this understanding, *Discovery* appears to herald a utopian future of gender and race equality. Martin-Green also says, "In *Star Trek's* utopian future, many of the gender issues have been rectified. It's common to see a woman of color in power" (Dockterman, 2017, p. 60).

We advocate that we should never stop attempting to make progress in pursuing gender equality as gender inequality is always an ongoing issue. Continually reviewing how gender has been represented in the past enables us to envision the future and will help us to make improvements. As Martin-Green's said: "We have to be at once celebratory of the change that has happened while at the same time yearning for more and realising that we're not done" (Dockterman, 2017, p. 60).

Critically Using the Declarative Mapping Sentence With Films and Television Programmes

In this book, we attempted to answer the question in regards to what is an appropriate research methodology that can be adopted in order to allow us to understand the ways in which women have been portrayed in science fiction television programmes and films. We also asked questions about what is a clear and transparent way of investigating how, if at all, women's roles in these forms of media have changed over time. In our attempts to answer these questions, we propose the use of the declarative mapping sentence methodology (Hackett, 2014, 2020, 2021).

Caveats and Future Research

The analyses we have reported constitute the first application of facet theory to the investigation of movies, television programmes or similar media. Within this genre, we have limited our purview to a particular geographical region: Western films and televisions. We do, however, acknowledge the limitations of these Western and Hollywood perspectives. However, in a short book such as ours, we made the decision to choose to these geographical regions in a desire to not introduce variation due to region in our analyses, as we would not be able to do this consideration justice. Future research will have to pursue a broader geographical consideration. It should also be remembered that our primary concerns and comments are methodological rather than about gender representation, per se. Indeed, in our writing, we acknowledge that gender is intersected with many other factors such as culture, race and geography. However, as the book is about what we consider to be appropriate method for investigating movies rather than a text about gender in films per se, we emphasised methodology.

This emphasis is demonstrated in the selection of films which were chosen to enable us to make methodological advances rather than producing a definitive depiction of the role of women in all science fiction films. We also recognise the importance of cultural factors and intersectionality within gender representation in attempting to locate and interpret lead women's roles in the selected movies. We consider the gendered gaze along with the notion that gender equity has not improved in a simple linear trajectory and we commented on these changes in reference to the facets in the mapping sentence. This is one of the strengths of the mapping sentence; in that, it specifies multiple criteria that may alter in different ways, and to different extents and at different times and then suggests how these features combine.

It is interesting to note that none of the female characters were rated as being represented by the elements of "bad in other way" for facet C (bad woman) and the element of partly independent and partly dependent for facet E (personal authority). It is interesting that, on these facets, only extremes were seen to be present. These elements could therefore have been deleted from the mapping sentence for our study. However, we decided to leave these in the mapping sentence, as we felt that other people rating the characters may have used these elements. Moreover, if the study was extended to include other movies and television film with other female characters, then the elements may have been useful.

It should be noted at this point that, in this book, we have been concerned with how women have been cast in science fiction media. We openly acknowledge that this focus of attention implicitly supports the binary classification of gender. The emphasis of a binary definition of gender is in no way an aim of our writing. We acknowledge the necessity to address and enhance more realistic forms of gender portrayal. Future research into gender representation in movies and television productions must acknowledge the over-simplistic notion of the binary differentiation of men and women.

A significant part of the research we report has involved the assembly of profiles of the female actors in our chosen movies. These profiles were generated initially based upon a review of writing on films and then were incorporated into the mapping sentence. We have adapted our declarative mapping sentence in a reflexive manner to each film. The profiles, and the criteria for their generation, are hypotheses that are contained in the mapping sentence and are supported/refuted/modified through research. We believe that our research has helped to generate novel ideas and inspirations for researchers who are interested in developing a greater understanding of films and television. The strength and utility of the declarative mapping sentence approach will become more apparent, as it is used by others to guide their studies to address other genres and aspects of television and film productions.

References

Doane, M.A. (1991) *Femme Fatales: Feminism, Film Theory, Psychoanalysis*, London: Routledge.

Dockterman, E. (2017) In a Quantum Leap, Star Trek Becomes a Female Enterprise, *Time Off*, 59–60.

Hackett, P.M.W. (2014) *Facet Theory and the Mapping Sentence: Evolving Philosophy, Use and Applications*, Basingstoke: Palgrave McMillan Publishers.

Hackett, P.M.W. (2020) *Declarative Mapping Sentences in Qualitative Research: Theoretical, Linguistic, and Applied Usages*, London: Routledge.

Hackett, P.M.W. (2021) *Facet Theory and the Mapping Sentence: Evolving Philosophy, Use and Declarative Applications* (second, revised and enlarged edition), Basingstoke: Palgrave McMillan Publishers

Jonsson, L., Nilsson, A.-M., and Andersson, G. (1994) *Musiken i Sverige. Från forntid till stormaktstidens slut 1720*, Stockholm: Fischer & Co.

Jung, C.G. (ed.) (1968) *Man and His Symbols*, New York: Dell Publishing Co., Inc.

Longworth, T.C., and Tice, P. (2003) *A Survey of Sex & Celibacy in Religion*, San Diego: The Book Tree, 61. Originally published as The Devil a Monk Would Be: A Survey of Sex & Celibacy in Religion (1945)

Manion, D., and Ursini, J. (2009) *Femme Fatale: Cinema's Most Unforgettable Lethal Ladies*, Lanham, MD: Rowman Littlefield.

Scaraffia, G. (2009) *Femme Fatale*, Firenze: Vallecchi Publishers.

Index

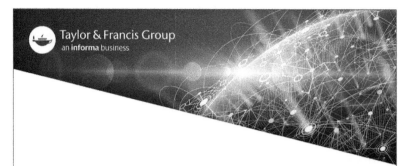

www.ingramcontent.com/pod-product-compliance
Ingram Content Group UK Ltd.
Pitfield, Milton Keynes, MK11 3LW, UK
UKHW020425010325
455677UK00029B/1009